Official Guide to the

Wales Coast Path: Carmarthen Bay and Gower

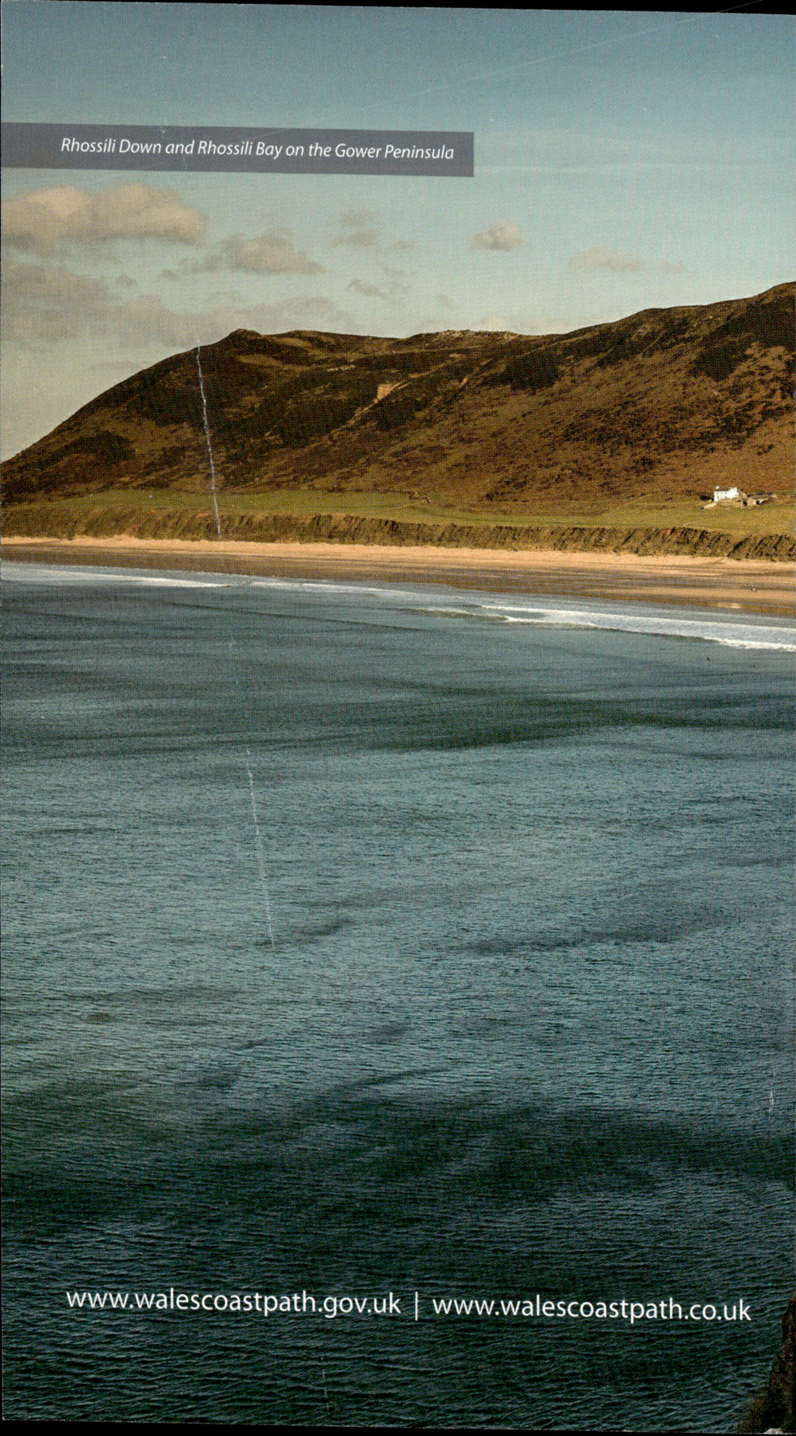

Rhossili Down and Rhossili Bay on the Gower Peninsula

Esta obra se terminó de imprimir
en el mes de noviembre de 2025,
en los talleres de Litográfica Ingramex S.A. de C.V.,
Ciudad de México.

Official Guide to the

Wales Coast Path
Carmarthen Bay and Gower

Tenby to Swansea
131 miles/ 210 kilometres of
superb coastal walking

Harri Garrod Roberts

Northern Eye

www.northerneyebooks.co.uk

Text: Harri Garrod Roberts

Series editor: Tony Bowerman

Introductory section: Tony Bowerman

Photographs: © Crown copyright (2015/2021) Visit Wales, discovercarmarthenshire.com, Carmarthenshire County Museum, Woodland Trust, Harri Garrod Roberts and Tracy Burton, Huw Davies, Paul Edwards/Aspects of Wales, Marc Evans/ffotomarc@civitascymru.co.uk, Phil Fitzsimmons, Paula J James, Mari Owen, Steve Wassell, Steve Young, Shutterstock, Dreamstime, Fotolia, Wikimedia Commons

Design: Carl Rogers

© Northern Eye Books Limited 2015/2021

Harri Garrod Roberts has asserted his rights under the Copyright, Designs and Patents Act, 1988 to be identified as the author of this work. All rights reserved.

This book contains mapping data licensed from the Ordnance Survey with the permission of the Controller of Her Majesty's Stationery Office.

All maps based on the 1:50,000 Landranger

© Crown copyright 2015/2021. All rights reserved. Licence number 100047867

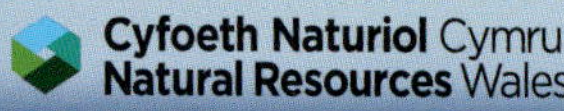

ISBN **978-1-908632-99-9**

A CIP catalogue record for this book is available from the British Library

@wales_coast_path
@Northerneyebooks

www.northerneyebooks.co.uk | www.walescoastpath.co.uk

Important Advice: The route described in this book is undertaken at the reader's own risk. Walkers should take into account their level of fitness, wear suitable footwear and clothing, and carry food and water. It is also advisable to take the relevant OS mapping with you in case you get lost and leave the area covered by our maps.

Whilst every care has been taken to ensure the accuracy of the route directions, the publishers cannot accept responsibility for errors or omissions, or for changes in the details given. Nor can the publisher and copyright owners accept responsibility for any consequences arising from the use of this book.

If you find any inaccuracies in either the text or maps, please write or email us at the addresses below. Thank you.

Acknowledgements: Warm thanks are due to everyone who helped make this book a reality. Thank you, in particular, to Natural Resources Wales' officer Quentin Grimley, Kelly Shefford, Carmarthenshire Countryside Business and Conservation Manager, Chris Dale, Swansea Countryside Access Team Leader, Theresa Nolan, Pembrokeshire Coast National Trail Officer, and Tricia Cottnam, Wales Coast Path Officer (South). Thanks, too, to the many tourism officers, museum and library staff, Wales on View picture researchers, freelance photographers, and everyone else who has played their part. Thank you, too, to Vivienne Crow for her Tenby to Amroth directions. And, finally, thanks to Steve Plant, end-to-end walker, for his passionate quote explaining why the Wales Coast Path is so special.

First published in 2015
This new, revised edition published 2021

Northern Eye Books Limited
Tattenhall, Cheshire CH3 9PX

Email: tony@northerneyebooks.co.uk

For trade and sales enquiries, please call 01928 723 744

Contents

Official Guides to the Wales Coast Path

The Official Guides to the Wales Coast Path are endorsed by **Natural Resources Wales,** the body responsible for coordinating the development of the route. The guides split the Path into seven main sections with a guide for each. Together, they cover the entire 870-mile Path from the outskirts of Chester in the north to Chepstow in the south.

For details of the full range of Official Guides to the Wales Coast Path, see: **www.walescoastpath.gov.uk/plan-your-trip/guidebooks.aspx**

Wales Coast Path
Discover the shape of a nation

Wales is the largest country in the world with a continuous path around its entire coast. The **Wales Coast Path** promises 870 miles/1400 kilometres of unbroken coastal walking, from the outskirts of Chester in the north to Chepstow in the south. Along the way you'll experience the very best of Wales: stunning scenery, stirring history, Welsh culture, and wildlife in abundance. If you tackle only one big walk in your life, make it this one. It's unmissable.

Conwy Mountain, Conwy

Llanddwyn Island lighthouse, Anglesey

Bottlenose dolphins

Caernarfon Castle, Gwynedd

Castle Hotel, Aberaeron, Ceredigion

'Green Bridge of Wales', Pembrokeshire

Rhossili Bay, Gower

Little egrets

Millennium Centre, Cardiff

Chepstow Castle, Gwent

Wales Coast Path
An 870-mile coastal adventure

When the **Wales Coast Path** opened in May 2012, Wales became the largest country in the world with a continuous path around its entire coast. Walkers can now enjoy unparalleled coastal walking around the Welsh seaboard from top to bottom: from the outskirts of the ancient walled city of Chester, on the Dee estuary, in the north, to the pretty market town of Chepstow, on the Severn Estuary, in the south.

The official, signposted and waymarked path covers roughly 870 miles/1400 kilometres and starts and finishes close to the ends of the historic 180 mile/285 kilometre Offa's Dyke National Trail. This means keen walkers

Worms Head, on the Gower Peninsula

can make a complete circumnavigation of Wales; a total distance of around 1,050 miles/1,690 kilometres. Ever keen for a new challenge, a few hardy walkers had already completed the full circuit within months of the Wales Coast Path's opening.

But whether you choose to walk the whole Path in one go, in occasional sections, or a few miles at a time, you're in for a real treat. There's something new around every corner, and you'll discover places that can only be reached on foot. Visually stunning and rich in both history and wildlife, the Path promises ever-changing views, soaring cliffs and spacious beaches, sea caves and arches, wildflowers, seabirds, seals and dolphins, as well as castles, cromlechs, coves and coastal pubs. It's a genuinely special landscape.

This visual and ecological richness is recognised nationally and internationally. In fact, the Wales Coast Path runs through 1 Marine Nature Reserve, 1 Geopark, 2 National Parks, 3 Areas of Outstanding Natural Beauty, 3 World Heritage Sites, 7 official and unofficial nudist beaches, 11 National Nature Reserves, 14 Heritage Coasts, 17 Special Protection Areas, 21 Special Areas of Conservation, 23 Historic Landscapes, 42 Blue Flag beaches, and 111 marine Sites of Special Scientific Interest. Large stretches of coast are also managed and protected by Wildlife Trusts, the RSPB and the National Trust.

Long-distance walkers will enjoy the unbroken path, the solitude, the coast's constantly changing moods and the back-to-nature challenge. Holiday and weekend walkers can recharge their batteries, see something new, and regain a necessary sense of perspective. Families can potter, play and explore. And locals can walk the dog, jog, get fit and rediscover their home patch. Whatever your preferences, the Wales Coast Path promises something for everyone.

" In 62 days of walking, I experienced stunning scenery, some amazing history and some intriguing folklore. Dig out your walking boots and enjoy all the Wales Coast Path has to offer."

Steve Plant, end-to-end charity walker, Spring 2014

All or Part?

So, what's the best way to walk the Wales Coast Path? The 870 mile/1400 kilometre route covers the whole of the Welsh seaboard and is the longest and probably the best of all Britain's long-distance challenges.

But of course, not everyone has the time, energy or inclination to walk it all at once. Instead, most people start with a short stretch, discover they love it, and come back for more.

Section by section

1 North Wales Coast

2 Isle of Anglesey

3 Llŷn Peninsula

4 Cardigan Bay/Ceredigion

5 Pembrokeshire Coast Path

6 Carmarthen Bay & Gower

7 South Wales Coast

1. North Wales Coast

Chester to Bangor
80 miles/125 kilometres
7 Day Sections

Undulating coast. Vast Dee estuary, traditional seaside towns, limestone headland, and Conwy mountain

2. Isle of Anglesey

Circuit of island from Menai Bridge
125 miles/200 kilometres
12 Day Sections

Grand coastal scenery from tidal straits to bays, estuaries, dunes and cliffs. Area of Outstanding Natural Beauty

3. Llŷn Peninsula

Bangor to Porthmadog
110 miles/180 kilometres
9 Day Sections

Unspoilt peninsula with bays, coves and cliffs, tipped by Bardsey Island. Area of Outstanding Natural Beauty

4. Cardigan Bay/Ceredigion

Porthmadog to Cardigan
140 miles/225 kilometres
12 Day Sections

Low-lying dunes and big estuaries followed by steeper, grassy sea cliffs with dramatic coves and bays

5. Pembrokeshire

Cardigan to Tenby/Amroth
185 miles/300 kilometres
14 Day Sections

Varied, beautiful, popular. The Pembrokeshire Coastal Path is a National Trail and coastal National Park

6. Carmarthen Bay & Gower

Tenby to Swansea
131 miles/210 kilometres
12 Day Sections

Long sandy beaches, tidal estuaries, dramatic rocky coast. Area of Outstanding Natural Beauty

7. South Wales Coast

Swansea to Chepstow
115 miles/185 kilometres
11 Day Sections

Traditional beach resorts, seafaring and industrial landscapes. Heritage Coast, National Nature Reserves

Limestone splendour: *A dramatic road runs around the Great Orme, on the North Wales coast*

Wales: Top to bottom

Walking the whole 870 miles/1400 kilometres of the Wales Coast Path in one go is an increasingly popular challenge. Some people have even run all the way. By a curious coincidence, the overall distance is almost exactly the same as Britain's famous top-to-bottom route, from John o' Groats to Land's End — a very long way.

The Wales Coast Path will take you from the outskirts of Chester down the broad Dee estuary, along the North Wales coast with its traditional seaside resorts and impressive limestone headlands at Little and Great Orme, past Conwy Castle, over Conwy Mountain and on along the wooded Menai Straits. The Path then loops around the rugged, offshore Isle of Anglesey, or Ynys Môn, passes the walled town of Caernarfon and its castle before heading around the remote Llŷn Peninsula with Bardsey Island balanced at its tip. From Criccieth and Porthmadog the Path pushes south past Harlech castle — kissing the western rim of the Snowdonia National Park — and on down the majestic sweep of Cardigan Bay with its beautiful, open estuaries. It then rounds Pembrokeshire — Britain's only coastal National Park — with

its sparkling bays and lofty cliffs. Striding through Carmarthenshire and crossing the wide Towy and Tâf estuaries, the Path curves around the lovely Gower Peninsula into Swansea Bay. Beyond the striking Glamorgan Heritage Coast, the Path runs along the Cardiff Bay waterfront to Cardiff, the lively capital of Wales. From there, it's only a short stretch alongside the broad Severn estuary to the pretty market town of Chepstow on the Welsh-English border and the southern end of the Wales Coast Path.

Only the fittest, most determined walkers can hope to complete the entire Path in 6-7 weeks, averaging 20 or so miles a day.

At a more leisurely pace — allowing time to soak up the atmosphere and enjoy the views, and with regular pauses to watch the wildlife, swim, enjoy a quiet drink or visit some of the fascinating places along the way — you should allow around 3 months for the whole trip.

Remember, though, the Wales Coast Path is a challenging route with plenty of rough ground, narrow paths and ups-and-downs (an overall total ascent and descent of 95,800 feet/ 29,200 metres). There are tempting detours and places to see along the way, too. So it's perhaps best to plan slightly shorter and more realistic daily distances than you might ordinarily cover.

You should also allow extra time for the unexpected, to rest or to hole up in bad weather. As a rule of thumb, it's better to be ahead of schedule, with time to enjoy the experience, rather than always having to push ahead to reach the next overnight stop.

The Official Guidebooks in this series break the path down into seven main sections (see the map on page 10), each of which is then sub-divided into carefully-planned 'Day Sections' — usually averaging around 10-15 miles each. These typically start and finish either in, or near easy-to-reach towns, villages or settlements, many of them on bus routes, and with shops, pubs, restaurants, cafés and places to stay nearby.

No matter how long it takes, walking the whole of the Wales Coast Path is a real achievement. For most of us, it would be the walk of a lifetime.

Walking around Wales a bit at a time

Yet, understandably, most people don't want to walk the whole path in one go. Instead, they prefer to do it bit by bit, often over several years: during annual and bank holidays, over long weekends, or as the whim takes them. Done in this leisurely fashion, the walk becomes a project to ponder, plan, and take pleasure in.

A popular way to enjoy the path is to book a short holiday close to a section of the path, and do a series of day walks along the surrounding coast, returning to your base each night.

South Stack lighthouse, on the north-west coast of Anglesey

Walking heaven: *Walkers above Black Rock Sands on the Llŷn Peninsula*

Some people like to catch a train (especially along the North Wales Coast), bus or taxi to the start of their day's walk and then walk back (see the information at the start of each day section).

Another approach is to drive to the end of your planned section and then get a pre-booked local taxi to take you back to the start; this costs only a few pounds and lets you walk in one direction at your own pace.

If you're planning to walk a section over several days before returning to your starting point by bus or train, call Traveline Cymru on 0800 464 00 00 or visit **www.traveline.cymru** for help with timetables and itineraries.

Best time to go?

Britain's main walking season runs from Easter to the end of September. Although the Wales Coast Path is delightful throughout the year, the best walking weather tends to be in late spring as well as early and late summer.

Although the Easter holiday is busy, spring is otherwise a quiet time of year. The days are lengthening and the weather getting steadily warmer. Migrant birds and basking sharks are returning to Wales from farther south. The weather is also likely to be dry.

Early summer is ideal for walking. May and June enjoy the greatest

Sacred Isle?: *Looking across the Sound to Bardsey Island, or Ynys Enlli, at the tip of Llŷn*

number of sunshine hours per day (the average for May is 225 hours, and for June 210 hours) and the lowest rainfall of the year (average for May is 50mm, June is 51mm). You'll also have the accompaniment of a spectacular array of spring flowers and the chance to see breeding sea birds at their best.

High summer is the busiest season, particularly during the school holidays in July and August. Both the beaches and the Coast Path are likely to be packed in places. Finding somewhere to stay at short notice can be tricky, too — so it's best to book well in advance. However, the long sunny days are certainly attractive, and you can often walk in shorts and a T-shirt.

By September most visitors have returned home, and you'll have the Coast Path largely to yourself. The weather remains good and the sea is still warm enough for swimming. Sunny days often stretch into September, with the first of the winter storms arriving in late September and October. Autumn also means the coastal trees and bracken are slowly turning from green to red, orange and gold.

Winter brings shorter, colder days with less sunlight and other disadvantages: unpredictable weather, stormy seas, high winds and even gales

along with closed cafés and accommodation. But for experienced walkers, the cooler days can bring peace and solitude and a heightened sense of adventure.

Welsh weather

Like the rest of Britain, Wales is warmed by the Gulf Stream's ocean current and enjoys a temperate climate. This is particularly true of the country's west coast. Because Wales lies in the west of Britain, the weather is generally mild but damp. Low pressure fronts typically come in off the Irish Sea from the west and southwest, hitting the coast first and then moving inland to the east. This means rain and wet weather can occur at any time of year, so you should always take good waterproofs and spare clothes with you.

For more weather or a five-day forecast, visit **www.metoffice.gov.uk** or **www.bbc.com/weather**. Several premium-rate national 'Weatherlines' give up-to-date forecasts, and the Snowdonia and Pembrokeshire National Parks websites provide local information too.

Which direction?

The Official Guide books give directions from north to south, starting in Chester and ending in Chepstow. This means walkers will enjoy the sun on their faces for much of the way. Most luggage transfer services also run in this direction. Nonetheless, the path can be tackled in either direction. It's just easier to go with the flow.

Which section?

Choosing which part of the Wales Coast Path to walk depends in part on where you live, how long you've got, and the kind of scenery you prefer.

Sections vary considerably. Arry Beresford-Webb, the first person to run the entire Path in 2012 said, 'I was stunned by the diversity of the Path. Each section felt like I was going through a different country.'

Some stretches are fairly wild, while others are more developed. Parts of the Isle of Anglesey, Llŷn Peninsula, Cardigan Bay and Pembrokeshire are often remote and away from large settlements. Other stretches, such as North Wales or the South Wales coast around Swansea, Cardiff and Newport are busier, and often close to popular seaside towns or industry.

The terrain varies too. Much of the North Wales coast is low-lying but punctuated with occasional headlands; as are much of Cardigan Bay, Carmarthen Bay, and parts of the Glamorgan Heritage Coast.

In contrast, the Isle of Anglesey, Llŷn Peninsula, Pembrokeshire and Gower are often rocky with high sea cliffs, dramatic headlands, offshore islands and intimate coves.

Self sufficient or supported?

The other key decision for walkers is whether to arrange everything yourself or let experts do it for you. For many people, devising their own itinerary and working out how to travel and where to stay is part of the fun. Others prefer to let one of the specialist walking holiday companies create the itinerary, book accommodation, arrange luggage transfers, meals, and side trips. The main companies are listed at the back of the book.

Accommodation

There are plenty of places to stay within easy reach of the Wales Coast Path all around Wales. Most walkers either camp or stay in bed and breakfast accommodation; usually a mix of the two. There are plenty of hostels and bunkhouses along the way but, unfortunately, they are too unevenly spaced to provide accommodation every night.

Accommodation may be fully booked during peak holiday seasons, so it's advisable to book well ahead. Local Tourist Information Centres (TICs) will often know all the local accommodation providers, know who has vacancies, and can help with booking. For late, or emergency on the spot bookings, it's also worth contacting the TICs listed at the start of each day section.

Backpacking

Backpacking adds an extra dimension to the walking experience: being outdoors for days at a time, watching the sunrise and sunset, gazing at the stars overhead without artificial light getting in the way. But don't underestimate how much a heavy pack can slow you down. The secret is to travel as light as possible; the lightest tent or bivvi bag, a lightweight sleeping bag and waterproofs, and a single change of clothes.

There are plenty of official campsites along the busier sections of the Wales Coast Path. However, many are on small farms and may not advertise. Elsewhere campsites are often few and far between, and may need searching for. During peak season some may also be full, so it's advisable to book ahead. But remember, most sites are closed during the winter (typically from November to Easter, and often longer).

The sandy mouth of the Dyfi Estuary reaches out towards Aberdovey

Coastal colour: *Yellow gorse and a deep blue sea near Strumble Head, in Pembrokeshire*

Unofficial 'wild camping' is a grey area. There is no legal right in England or Wales to 'wild camp' anywhere, including alongside the Path. Every scrap of land in Britain belongs to someone, and many landowners frown on campers. So it makes sense to ask before pitching.

Unofficially, however, overnight camping is usually tolerated, so long as you pitch a small tent unobtrusively in the evening, and pack up and leave early the next morning, without leaving a trace.

Alternatively, there are popular luggage transfer services on the more established stretches of the Path. For a small fee, they wiil pick up your rucksack and other bags and transport them to the end of your day's walk. A list of luggage transfer companies appears at the back of the book.

Clothes, boots and backpack

For those new to long-distance walking, it's worth emphasising the benefits of comfortable walking boots and suitable clothing. Walking continuously, day after day, puts extra pressures on your feet. Be prepared for changes in the weather too. Carry waterproofs and remember that several thin layers allow you to adjust your clothing as conditions change.

Checking the weather forecast before you set off each day will help you decide what to wear. If you're in the car, it's worth taking a selection of clothing for different conditions, and deciding what to wear and carry immediately before you start.

Onshore breezes can mask the strength of the sun. To avoid sunburn, or even sunstroke, remember to slap on some sunscreen and wear a hat.

Other things to take, depending on weight, include: maps, water bottle, lightweight walking poles, basic First Aid including plasters and antiseptic cream, penknife, head torch and spare batteries, chocolate, sweets or energy bars, toilet paper, a small camera, binoculars, mobile phone, and a pen and notebook. Don't forget some spare cash too; most places accept cards but finding a Cashpoint or somewhere that offers 'Cash Back' near the Path can be tricky.

Worms Head, on the Gower, stretches almost a mile out to sea

Beautiful bay: *Above Three Cliffs Bay, on the Gower Peninsula*

Food and drink

Although the official guidebooks try to start and end each day at places with amenities, some sections are nonetheless remote and may have few places to buy food or drink. This may be the case for several days in a row. So it makes sense to plan ahead and carry enough supplies with you.

Conversely, other sections are well supplied with shops, pubs, cafés, and takeaways, and these are indicated at the start of each Day Section.

Maps

The maps in this book are based on the Ordnance Survey Landranger 1:50,000 series, with the line of the Wales Coast Path highlighted in orange. The numbers on the maps correspond to those in the route description for each day section.

The best maps for walking are the larger scale, orange-covered Ordnance Survey Explorer 1:25,000 scale maps, which show additional features such as Access Land, field boundaries, springs and wells. Both scales of OS maps now have the official route of the Wales Coast Path marked on them: as a line composed of a series of red diamonds on the 1:50,000 Landranger maps, and green diamonds on the 1:25,000 Explorer maps.

Some walkers prefer to use digital mapping apps such as Viewranger.

The relevant maps for each Day Section are listed at the beginning of each chapter. The grid references given in this book for the start and finish of each Day Section are from the Ordnance Survey maps.

Route finding

For the most part, the Wales Coast Path follows a single official route. In a few places, there are both official and unofficial alternative routes. Otherwise, the path hugs the coast as far is practicably and legally possible, occasionally diverting inland around private estates, nature reserves, natural obstacles, estuaries, gunnery ranges and so on. The definitive route, and any occasional changes are notified on the official Wales Coast Path website.

The path uses a mixture of public rights of way: footpaths, bridleways and byways as well as lanes, open access land, beaches and some permissive paths. On most sections, the route is well-used and clear. In remote or under-used areas, however, walkers will need to pay closer attention to the maps and directions in this book.

Fingerposts and waymarkers

The Wales Coast Path is clearly signed and waymarked with its own distinctive logo: a white dragon-tailed seashell on a blue background surrounded by a yellow circlet bearing the words *'Llwybr Arfordir Cymru - Wales Coast Path'*. Look for the wood or metal fingerposts at main access points, in towns, on roadsides and lanes, and at key junctions.

Mumbles lighthouse and pier, on Swansea Bay

Way to go: *Oak signposts and waymarkers with the Wales Coast Path symbol mark the route*

Elsewhere the route is clearly waymarked with plastic roundels fixed to stiles, gateposts, fences and walls. In many places the Wales Coast Path waymarkers sit alongside others for already established routes — such as the Isle of Anglesey Coastal Path or the Pembrokeshire Coast Path National Trail. In some areas these local waymarkers are still more in evidence than the official Wales Coast Path ones; and on some stretches, waymarking remains patchy.

Official route waymarkers

Official alternative route waymarker

Alternative routes

Two sorts of alternative route are described in the guides. The first are the **official alternative routes** that avoid remote or challenging sections; and more attractive routes that, for example, provide better views or get farther away from motor traffic.

The second are our own **unofficial alternative routes**. Many of these are beach routes below the high water mark that by their nature are not permanently available, and so do not qualify as part of the 'official route'. Others are alternative high level routes or simply 'better' or more attractive, in our opinion. Both the **official** and **unofficial alternative routes** are shown on the maps in this book as a broken orange highlight.

Detours

The directions also describe **detours** to places of interest that we think you won't want to miss. These are usually short, off the main Path, there-and-back routes, typically of no more than a kilometre or so in each direction. Suggested detours can take you to anything from a special pub, castle or church to a stunning view or waterfall. If you've got the time, they bring an extra dimension to the walk. Detours are shown as a blue broken highlight.

Temporary diversions

There may be occasional or seasonal temporary inland diversions. The reasons for them vary from land management and public safety: forestry work, cliff falls, landslips and floods, to wildlife conservation: protecting seal breeding sites, bird roosts and nesting sites, and so on. Details of the latest permanent and temporary diversions can be found on the official Wales Coast Path website under 'Route Changes'. See **www.walescoastpath.gov.uk**

Tides and tide tables

As much as five percent of the Wales Coast Path runs along the foreshore, between mean high and low water. These sections are naturally affected by the tide. On the whole, the official Wales Coast Path avoids beaches and estuaries. However, beaches often provide time-honoured, direct and pleasant walking routes and are usually safely accessible, except for around 1½ hours either side of high tide. If the tide is in, or you're in any doubt, take the inland route instead.

Occasional streams and tidal creeks may also be crossed at low tide but be impassable at high water. So it is a good idea to carry tide tables with you and consult them before you set out each day. They are widely available for around £1 from coastal TICs, shops and newsagents.

Several websites also give accurate tidal predictions for locations around the UK, including downloadable five day predictions. Useful websites include: **www.bbc.com/weather/coast-and-sea/tide-tables**

Ancient layers: *Limestone cliffs at Nash Point on the Glamorgan Heritage Coast, South Wales*

Safety advice

If you're new to long-distance walking, or in one of the remoter areas, please remember:

- Wear walking boots and warm, waterproof clothing.
- Take food and drink.
- Mobile signals are patchy along much of the Path; let someone know where you are heading and when you expect to arrive.
- If you decide to walk along a beach, always check tide tables.
- Stay on the path and away from cliff edges.
- Take extra care in windy and/or wet conditions.
- Always supervise children and dogs.
- Follow local signs and diversions.

Emergencies

In an emergency, call 999 or 112 and ask for the service you require: Ambulance, Police, Fire or Coastguard.

Tell them your location as accurately as possible (give an OS grid reference, if possible; and look for named landmarks), how many people are in your party, and the nature of the problem.

Remember, though, that mobile signals may be poor or absent in some areas. Some coastal car parks and main beach access points have emergency telephones. Coastal pubs and shops may also have phones you can ask to use in an emergency.

Who manages the Path?

The Wales Coast Path is co-ordinated at a national level by Natural Resources Wales and managed on the ground by the sixteen local authorities and two National Parks through which it passes.

Funding has come from the Welsh Government, the European Regional Development Fund and the local authorities themselves.

For more details, see: **www.naturalresourceswales.gov.uk**

The Best of Carmarthen Bay & Gower

The **Carmarthenshire coast** stretches from the Pembrokeshire border to the **Gower Peninsula** and is dominated by the long arc of Carmarthen Bay. Wide, silty estuaries are a characteristic feature, but there are also sandy beaches as well as high cliffs and rocky coves. Look out for sea birds and enjoy the laid-back atmosphere of the county's coastal towns. South of Carmarthenshire is the Gower Peninsula, Britain's first designated Area of Outstanding Natural Beauty (AONB). Here you will enjoy an astonishing variety of coastal landscapes in one of the most stunningly beautiful areas in Britain.

Pendine Sands

Dylan Thomas sculpture

Wharley Point, near Llansteffan

Llansteffan Castle

Cefn Sidan sands

Rhossili Bay and Rhossili Down

'Helvetia' wreck, Rhossili Bay

Oxwich Bay and Great Tor

Mumbles lighthouse and pier

Maritime Quarter, Swansea

Carmarthen Bay & Gower
Part of the **Wales Coast Path**

Carmarthen Bay and the **Gower Peninsula** offer some of the finest coastal walking in South Wales, rivalling even the Pembrokeshire National Park for beauty and natural variety. The Gower Peninsula in particular is a place of stunning and astonishingly varied beauty, despite being little more than 15 miles long and 7 miles wide. But the attractions of the Carmarthenshire coast — its historic ports, peaceful estuaries and glorious sandy beaches — should not be overlooked either. Together, these two distinct areas comprise a fabulously diverse section of the Wales Coast Path.

Aerial view of Three Cliffs Bay, on Gower's south coast

Once seen, it is obvious why the Gower Peninsula was chosen as Britain's first designated Area of Outstanding Natural Beauty (AONB). The coastline of the peninsula has added protection as a Heritage Coast and is also the site of three National Nature Reserves. Many coastal commons on Gower are owned and managed by the National Trust. The Carmarthenshire coast enjoys fewer statutory protections, although Carmarthen Bay and the Burry Inlet have been designated Special Protection Areas for their international importance as a site for wintering sea birds.

The walking is as varied as the landscape, with the initial stretch between Tenby and Pendine being the toughest. Beyond Pendine, rugged cliffs give way to a landscape of sand and silt extending all the way to Gower's iconic Worms Head. The south Gower coast is wild and rocky and contains some of the most impressive limestone cliffs in Britain, as well as a number of popular and stunningly beautiful sandy bays. An easy stroll along the Swansea Bay cycle path concludes the section.

From start to finish, this is an inspiring and richly rewarding walk and should take around 10 to 12 days to complete. Don't miss it.

from *Taliesin in Gower* by Vernon Watkins, poet of Gower's landscape

Day Section	Distance	Start	Finish
Day Section 1 Tenby to Pendine	13 miles 20 km	S. Beach, Tenby SN 134 002	Pendine SN 233 079
Day Section 2 Pendine to St Clears	11 miles 17 km	Pendine SN 233 079	St Clears SN 281 153
Day Section 3 St Clears to Llansteffan	10 miles 16 km	St Clears SN 281 153	Llansteffan SN 352 104
Day Section 4 Llansteffan to Carmarthen	9 miles 15 km	Llansteffan SN 352 104	Carmarthen SN 411 198

Walking Carmarthen Bay & Gower

The Carmarthen Bay and Gower section of the Wales Coast Path runs for 131 miles/210 kilometres between Tenby and Swansea, and is split into twelve day sections. Each starts and finishes at or close to somewhere attractive and accessible with good facilities.

Day Section	Distance	Start	Finish
Day Section 5 Carmarthen to Kidwelly	14 miles 22 km	Carmarthen SN 411 198	Kidwelly SN 407 067
Day Section 6 Kidwelly to Burry Port	10 miles 17 km	Kidwelly SN 407 067	Burry Port SN 444 004
Day Section 7 Burry Port to Loughor	11 miles 17 km	Burry Port SN 444 004	Loughor SS 563 980
Day Section 8 Loughor to Llanmadoc	13 miles 21 km	Loughor SS 563 980	Llanmadoc SS 447 936
Day Section 9 Llanmadoc to Rhossili	10 miles 17 km	Llanmadoc SS 447 936	Rhossili SS 414 881
Day Section 10 Rhossili to Oxwich	12 miles 19 km	Rhossili SS 414 881	Oxwich SS 500 864
Day Section 11 Oxwich to Caswell Bay	9 miles 14 km	Oxwich SS 500 864	Caswell Bay SS 593 877
Day Section 12 Caswell Bay to Swansea Marina	9 miles 15 km	Caswell Bay SS 593 877	Swansea Marina SS 663 924

Distance chart for key locations along the path

In each row the cells to the left of the shaded diagonal (blank) give distances in **miles**; the cells to the right of the diagonal give distances in **kilometres**.

Miles → / ← **Kilometres**	Swansea Marina	Mumbles Head	Caswell Bay	Oxwich	Port Eynon	Rhossili	Llanmadoc	Pen-clawdd	Gowerton	Loughor	Llanelli	Burry Port	Pembrey C'try Pk	Kidwelly Station	Llansaint	Ferryside	Carmarthen	Llansteffan	St Clears	Laugharne	Pendine	Amroth	Saundersfoot	Tenby South Beach
Tenby S'th Beach	131	125	122	113	108	101	90	82	79	77	71	66	64	56	53	51	42	33	23	18	13	8	4	
Saundersfoot	126	120	117	108	104	96	86	77	75	73	66	62	59	52	49	46	38	29	19	14	8	3		7
Amroth	123	117	114	105	101	93	83	74	72	70	63	59	56	49	46	43	35	25	16	11	5		5	12
Pendine	118	112	109	100	96	88	78	69	67	65	58	54	51	44	41	38	30	20	11	6		8	13	20
Laugharne	112	107	104	95	90	83	72	64	61	59	52	48	45	38	35	33	24	15	5		9	17	22	29
St Clears	107	102	98	90	85	78	67	59	56	54	47	43	41	33	30	28	19	10		8	17	25	30	37
Llansteffan	98	92	89	80	75	68	57	49	46	44	38	33	31	23	20	18	9		16	24	33	41	46	53
Carmarthen	88	83	80	71	66	59	48	40	37	35	29	24	22	14	11	9		15	31	39	48	56	61	68
Ferryside	80	74	71	62	57	50	39	31	28	26	20	15	13	5	2		14	29	45	53	62	70	75	82
Llansaint	77	72	69	60	55	48	37	29	26	24	18	13	11	3		4	18	33	49	57	66	74	79	86
Kidwelly Station	71	69	66	57	52	45	34	26	23	21	15	10	8		4	8	22	37	53	61	70	78	83	90
Pembrey C'try Park	67	61	58	49	44	37	26	18	15	13	7	2		13	17	21	35	50	66	74	83	91	96	103
Burry Port	64	59	56	47	42	35	24	16	13	11	5		4	17	21	25	39	54	70	78	87	95	100	107
Llanelli	56	54	51	42	37	30	19	11	8	6		7	11	24	28	32	46	61	77	85	94	102	107	114
Loughor	53	48	45	36	31	24	13	5	2		10	17	21	34	38	42	56	71	87	95	104	112	117	124
Gowerton	52	46	43	34	29	22	11	3		3	13	20	24	37	41	45	59	74	90	98	107	115	120	127
Pen-clawdd	47	43	40	31	26	19	8		5	8	18	25	29	42	46	50	64	79	95	103	112	120	125	132
Llanmadoc	40	35	32	23	18	11		14	19	22	32	39	43	56	60	64	78	93	109	117	126	134	139	146
Rhossili	30	24	21	12	7		16	30	35	38	48	55	59	72	76	80	94	109	125	133	142	150	155	162
Port Eynon	23	17	14	5		12	28	42	47	50	60	67	71	84	88	92	106	121	137	145	154	162	167	174
Oxwich	18	12	9		8	20	36	50	55	58	68	75	79	92	96	100	114	129	143	152	161	169	175	182
Caswell Bay	9	3		14	22	33	50	64	68	71	82	89	93	105	110	114	128	143	158	166	176	181	189	196
Mumbles Head	6		3	19	27	39	55	69	74	76	87	94	98	111	115	119	133	148	163	171	181	189	194	201
Swansea Marina		9	15	29	36	48	65	79	83	86	97	103	108	120	124	128	142	157	173	181	190	198	203	210

Miles (row distances, left of diagonal) · **Kilometres** (row distances, right of diagonal)

Distances are approximate to the nearest mile/kilometre

Day Sections

1: Tenby to Pendine

Distance: 13 miles/20 kilometres

Terrain: A tough section. Wooded clifftops, quiet lanes and a former tramway provide relatively easy walking as far as Amroth and the Pembrokeshire/Carmarthenshire border. Beyond Amroth, the coast is a lot more rugged and there are numerous steep climbs and descents; be prepared.

Points of interest: Views of Caldey Island, Tenby, former tramway, seabird colonies, Iron Age forts, Marros Sands, Neolithic burial chambers, WWII defences in Morfa Bychan, views along Pendine Sands.

Note: Several pubs and cafés between Tenby and Amroth. Accommodation, pubs, cafés, takeaways and shop in Pendine.

2: Pendine to St Clears

Distance: 11 miles/17 kilometres

Terrain: Roadside walking for much of the route between Pendine and Laugharne; good-quality paths and tracks along Tâf Estuary between Coygen and Delacorse; tracks, field paths and roadside walking between Delacorse and St Clears.

Points of interest: Pendine Sands, site of early human habitation at Coygen

Tenby Old Town and harbour from the air

Quarry, Dylan's Birthday Walk, Laugharne, Laugharne Castle, Dylan Thomas' Boathouse, River Tâf.

Note: Accommodation, pubs, cafés, takeaways and shops in Laugharne and St Clears.

3: St Clears to Llansteffan

Distance: 10 miles/16 kilometres

Terrain: Mainly field paths with some lane walking; winding cliff path between Wharley Point and Llansteffan (optional beach route between Scott's Bay and Llansteffan).

Points of interest: St Clears Castle, Trefenty, St Michael's Church, St Teilo's Church, St David's pilgrim route, the King's Highway, spectacular sea and estuary views from Wharley Point, St Antony's Well, Llansteffan Castle.

Note: Accommodation, pubs, cafés and takeaway in Llansteffan.

4: Llansteffan to Carmarthen

Distance: 9 miles/15 kilometres

Terrain: Tracks, field paths and minor roads, including two long, steep climbs (the first along a sunken track from Llansteffan, the second up a lane near Llangain); woodland walk through Green Castle Woods; roadside walking parallel to the B4312; level riverside path into Carmarthen.

Llansteffan Castle at the mouth of the Towy Estuary

Points of interest: Llansteffan, estuary views, St Cain's Church, Green Castle Woods Nature Reserve, Carmarthen town and castle.

Note: Plenty of accommodation, banks, pubs, cafés, takeaways and shops in Carmarthen.

5: Carmarthen to Kidwelly

Distance: 14 miles/22 kilometres

Terrain: Roadside walking along the A484, then along a minor road to Croesyceiliog; tracks, field paths and narrow country lanes to Ferryside; steep climb through fields to Llansaint followed by steep descent on track; busy minor road and cycle path into centre of Kidwelly.

Points of interest: The ferries between Ferryside and Llansteffan are running again (**www.carmarthenbayferries.co.uk**), Pengay Farm, medieval hilltop village (Llansaint), Kidwelly Castle.

Note: Accommodation, pubs, cafés, takeaways and shops in Kidwelly.

6: Kidwelly to Burry Port

Distance: 10 miles/17 kilometres

Terrain: Entirely level section, mainly along Route 4 of the National Cycle Network. Minor road to Kidwelly Quay and then along the towpath of the Kymer Canal; short section of roadside walking, then concrete track across marshy grazing to Pembrey Forest and out onto Cefn Sidan Sands. Purpose-built cycle path through the Millennium Coastal Park to Burry Port.

Points of interest: Kidwelly Quay, Glan yr Afon Nature Reserve, Kymer Canal, Pembrey Forest and Nature Reserve, Cefn Sidan Sands, Pembrey Country Park and visitor centre, Pembrey Burrows and Saltings Nature Reserve, Millennium Coastal Park, Pembrey Harbour, Burry Port Marina.

Note: Accommodation, bank, pubs, cafés, takeaways and shops in Burry Port.

7: Burry Port to Loughor

Distance: 11 miles/17 kilometres

Terrain: Easy, level walking along Route 4 of the National Cycle Network, mainly within the Millennium Coastal Park. Two sections of parallel path provide a respite from the tarmac. A residential road in Bynea leads to the Loughor Bridge, which is crossed by a pavement alongside the A484.

Points of interest: Burry Port Marina, Millennium Coastal Park, estuary views, Ashpits Pond and Pwll Lagoon Nature Reserve, Discovery Centre in

Beautiful bay: *Backed by Rhossili Down, Rhossili Bay is often voted the best beach in Wales*

Llanelli, North Dock Dunes Nature Reserve, industrial heritage around Llanelli, abandoned village in Machynys, Trostre Steelworks, National Wetland Centre Wales, Loughor Bridge.

Note: Accommodation, banks, pubs, cafés, takeaways and shops in Llanelli; limited accommodation and shop in Loughor.

8: Loughor to Llanmadoc

Distance: 13 miles/21 kilometres

Terrain: Cycle path, bridleway and minor roads to Gowerton; mixture of undulating field paths and level cycle path to Pen-clawdd; roadside walking to Crofty; marshland track and unfenced minor road to Llanrhidian; mainly level field paths to Landimore; rough marshland track from Landimore to Llanmadoc.

Points of interest: Loughor Castle, former docks in Pen-clawdd, Llanrhidian Marsh, views of Cilifor Top and Iron Age fort, historic church and mill in Llanrhidian, Llanrhidian Hill Nature Reserve, Hambury Wood Nature Reserve, Weobley Castle, Bovehill Castle, Landimore Marsh SSSI, North Hill Tor, Burry

Pill, Lucas Nature Reserve.

Note: Accommodation, pub, café and shop in Llanmadoc; more services available in Gowerton, Pen-clawdd, Crofty and Llanrhidian.

9: Llanmadoc to Rhossili

Distance: 10 miles/17 kilometres

Terrain: Varied section combining marshland, dunes, cliffs and forests — not to mention some of Gower's finest beaches. Old sea wall from Llanmadoc across marshes to Whiteford Burrows and choice of official routes. Longer route crosses dunes and marshland to Whiteford point, then tracks back along Whiteford Sands; shorter route heads straight for Hills Tor (optional low tide route along beach to Broughton). Sand dune cliffs between Broughton and Burry Holms; beach walk and bridlepath along base of Rhossili Downs to Rhossili (optional route along beach or over top of downs).

Points of interest: Cwm Ivy Marsh, Whiteford National Nature Reserve, Whiteford Point Lighthouse, Cwm Ivy Tor, Broughton Bay, Blue Pool, Culver Hole (cave containing Bronze Age human remains), Burry Holms, Rhossili Bay, Rhossili Down, spectacular sea views, St Mary's Church.

Rocky snout: *Worms Head stretches more than a mile out to sea*

Note: Accommodation, pub and café in Rhossili.

10: Rhossili to Oxwich

Distance: 12 miles/19 kilometres

Terrain: Rugged coastal path with possible side-trip across tidal causeway to Worms Head. Grassy cliff tops and narrow, steep-sided valleys between Worms Head and Port-Eynon; mainly level path below low limestone cliffs to Oxwich Point (one short, inland detour due to coastal erosion); steep climb and descent with numerous steps in Oxwich Wood.

Points of interest: National Trust visitor centre, views along Rhossili Bay, Worms Head, Gower Coast National Nature Reserve, Paviland Cave, Longhole Cave, Overton Cliff Nature Reserve, Culver Hole, Port-Eynon Point Nature Reserve, remains of salt house in Port-Eynon, Oxwich National Nature Reserve, St Illtyd's Church.

Note: Accommodation, pubs and cafés in Port-Eynon and Oxwich

11: Oxwich to Caswell Bay

Distance: 9 miles/14 kilometres

Terrain: Dunes, woods and grassy cliff tops lead to steep, sandy descent into Three Cliffs Bay and stepping stones across Pennard Pill (optional beach routes between Oxwich and Three Cliffs Bay). Steep, sandy paths climb out of Three Cliffs Bay onto high, grassy cliffs extending east to Pwlldu Head. Steep descent on bridle track to Pwlldu Bay; narrow, winding path along rugged coastline to Caswell Bay.

Points of interest: Oxwich National Nature Reserve, Nicholaston Wood, Neolithic burial chamber and the remains of a medieval church and ringwork castle in Penmaen Burrows, Three Cliffs Bay, Pennard Castle, Minchin Hole Cave, Pwlldu Head, Pwlldu and Bishopston Valley Nature Reserve, Redley Cliff Wildlife Trust Reserve, Caswell Bay.

Note: Accommodation, shop and café in Pennard; café at Caswell Bay but little else. Buses from Caswell Bay to Oystermouth and Swansea.

12: Caswell Bay to Swansea Marina

Distance: 9 miles/15 kilometres

Terrain: Undulating but well-surfaced path from Caswell Bay to Limeslade Bay; short section of roadside walking to Mumbles Head; steps down to pier; Swansea Bay cycle path from Mumbles to Swansea Marina (optional beach walk for part of way).

Points of interest: Caswell Bay, Langland Bay, Mumbles Head, Mumbles Hill Nature Reserve, The Mumbles, Oystermouth Castle, Clyne Gardens, Blackpill (wildlife centre and SSSI), Clyne Valley Country Park, Marina Towers Observatory, National Waterfront Museum, Tawe Barrage, Swansea Marina, Dylan Thomas Centre.

Note: Cafés in Langland and Limeslade; plenty of accommodation, banks, pubs, cafés, takeaways and shops in the Mumbles and Swansea.

Caswell Bay and the Mumbles

Limited for time? — Gower in a nutshell

If you have limited time to explore this section of the Wales Coast Path — perhaps a weekend, or even just a day — then these key parts of the path are unmissable.

For a superb one-day walk, the section between Llanmadoc and Rhossili (Day Section 9) is about as good as it gets. Join the Coast Path at Llanmadoc and follow it around Whiteford Point. Return directly to Llanmadoc for a shorter loop, or continue along the Coast Path to Rhossili Bay.

Alternatively, for a superb two-day walk, the section between Rhossili and the Mumbles is recommended. This takes in the entire rugged coast of south Gower and, tide permitting, also includes the option of an excursion across the rocky causeway to Worms Head. The views on Day 2 are equally stunning, with the iconic Three Cliffs Bay being a particular delight.

Best day walk
Dunes, beaches and downland on Gower's stunning western edge
Llanmadoc to Rhossili: 10 miles/ 17 kilometres
From Llanmadoc (Day Section 9), join the Coast Path near Cwm Ivy and follow it out to the tip of Whiteford Point. Return to Cwm Ivy via Whiteford Sands or continue along the Coast Path to Rhossili. There is a car park at the western edge of Llanmadoc and a larger, National Trust car park in Rhossili. More ambitious walkers can return to Llanmadoc over the tops of Rhossili Down and Llanmadoc Hill.

Cwm Ivy and Whiteford Sands, Gower

Best weekend walk
Gower's rugged southern coast between Rhossili and the Mumbles

Rhossili to the Mumbles: 24 miles/ 39 kilometres
Day One: From Rhossili (Day Section 10), follow the Coast Path to Worms Head and then along the south Gower coast to Port-Eynon and Oxwich.

Day Two: From Oxwich (Day Section 11), follow the south Gower coast to Caswell Bay and the start of Day Section 12. Continue along the popular tarmac path linking Caswell, Langland and the Mumbles.

There is a car park at Rhossili and regular summer buses from Swansea.

Three Cliffs Bay, Gower

A brief history of
Carmarthen Bay & Gower

Carmarthen Bay and Gower are rich in monuments and other reminders of the past

Stone tools discovered along the **Carmarthen Bay** and **Gower** coast confirm that Neanderthal people were living in the region as early as 70,000 years ago. Over the next 40,000 years, Neanderthals became extinct and were replaced throughout Europe by modern humans. The earliest remains of a modern human to be found in Britain — a partial male skeleton wrongly dubbed the 'Red Lady of Paviland' — come from Gower and have been dated to around 33,000 years ago. At that time, the sea level would have been some 80 metres lower than it is today and Paviland Cave would have been located on the edge of a large tundra plain.

Following the end of the last Ice Age, approximately 12,000 years ago, sea levels began to rise rapidly, forming over the next few thousand years the distinctive shape of the Gower Peninsula and Carmarthen Bay.

Arthur's Stone is all that remains of a Neolithic burial chamber above Llanrhidian, Gower

The first farmers

Around 4000 BC, the hunter-gatherer societies of the Mesolithic or Middle Stone Age were replaced by communities who grew crops and raised domesticated animals. These Neolithic or New Stone Age people were the first to make a significant impact on the Welsh landscape through the clearing of forests. They also built large, megalithic burial chambers, still visible at a number of locations along the Carmarthenshire and Gower coast.

Around 2500 BC, the spread of people and new metal-making technologies from continental Europe heralded the start of the Bronze Age in Britain. Bronze tools were quicker at clearing land for farming, but they also made better weapons of war. The use of iron after 500 BC led to a further intensification of warfare. Possibly as a result of population pressures, the Iron Age appears to have been a period of almost endemic raiding between different tribal groupings, with numerous defensive forts being constructed on hilltops and coastal promontories. The larger hillforts, such as those on north Gower, would have acted as a refuge for both people and livestock during times of raids, but they may also have served as a focal point for tribal administration and religious ceremony.

Gower hillfort: *Ramparts of the Iron Age defended settlement on Hardings Down, Gower*

Roman and post-Roman Wales

The arrival of the Romans in the first century AD led to the foundation of a town, *Moridunum*, on the site of present-day Carmarthen. This served as an administrative centre for the local *Demetae* tribe, who, once they had submitted to Roman rule, were allowed to form a *civitas* or self-governing republic. However, outside *Moridunum* there appears to have been little disruption of indigenous cultural and agricultural practices.

The withdrawal of the last Roman legions from Britain at the beginning of the fifth century created a political vacuum, with a number of petty kingdoms jostling for control over the region. The western half of Carmarthenshire up to the River Towy was dominated by the Kingdom of Dyfed. To the east was a region known collectively as Ystrad Tywi ('Vale of the River Towy'), which was repeatedly fought over by the neighbouring kingdoms of Dyfed, Ceredigion and Glywysing (Glamorgan). One of the commotes or administrative subdivisions of this territory was Gŵyr, a name still used today as the Welsh form of Gower. In the tenth century, Dyfed, Ceredigion and Ystrad Tywi were unified by Hywel Dda into a larger kingdom called Deheubarth. This was roughly the situation when the Normans launched their first full-scale invasion of Wales at the beginning of the twelfth century.

Normans in Gower

The decisive date for Gower is 1106, when Henry, the Earl of Warwick, was given free rein by Henry I to seize Gŵyr from the Welsh. By the time of his death in 1116, the earl had thrown up a line of motte-and-bailey castles along the length of the commote and begun the process of ethnically cleansing the rich agricultural lands of the Gower Peninsula by replacing their original Welsh inhabitants with English peasants from Devon and Somerset. Other coastal regions of Deheubarth were assaulted about the same time and English settlements proliferated around the shores of Carmarthen Bay.

Nevertheless, for at least a century, Norman rule remained precarious, with the Welsh making repeated attempts to regain their lost territory; between 1113 and 1217 there were at least half a dozen Welsh assaults on marcher boroughs, many of them devastating. By 1300, Wales's last independent prince had been defeated, but sporadic raids continued to take place throughout the fourteenth century, culminating in a final full-scale rebellion by Owain Glyndŵr (1400–10).

Following the defeat of Glyndŵr, Wales entered a more peaceful period in which the administration of the country became tied ever closer to that of England. In 1535, the last remaining marcher lordships were abolished by the so-called Act of Union: Gower was transferred to the newly created county of Glamorgan, while the rest of Ystrad Tywi and the eastern part of Dyfed were united to form Carmarthenshire. In this more peaceful era, the region's castles were either allowed to fall into decay or were rebuilt as manor houses by their new aristocratic owners. There was further bloody violence during the Civil War (1642–51), but the long-term trend was towards greater peace and prosperity.

Ruined medieval Llansteffan Castle guards the mouth of the Towy estuary

Salt of the earth?: *Ruined salt house on the point at Port-Eynon near Swansea*

Peace and prosperity

By the sixteenth century, the port of Carmarthen, now the largest town in Wales, had become central to the local economy. Along with other neighbouring ports (most notably Kidwelly), Carmarthen enabled the region's farmers, weavers, wool makers and corn millers to export their goods to far-flung markets. Fishing was also an important industry in the region, along with illegal and semi-legal activities such as smuggling and wrecking. Another important coastal industry was the production of sea salt – one of the only means of preserving meat prior to refrigeration. There was an extensive salt house at Port Eynon on the south Gower coast, indicating that the village was a major trader in the commodity in the early modern period. Some small-scale industrial activity also began during this period: limestone quarrying along the south Gower cliffs and mining for coal in southern Carmarthenshire and along the eastern edge of the Gower Peninsula.

Extractive industries were increasingly important by the start of the nineteenth century. Coal and tinplate were already being exported from Kidwelly during the eighteenth century, assisted by a canal built by local industrialist

Thomas Kymer. In 1832, the canal was extended to newly constructed docks in Burry Port, while by the end of the century the neighbouring town of Llanelli had been dubbed 'Tinopolis'. Along the eastern edge of the Gower Peninsula, where coal lay close to the surface, there was a proliferation of primitive bell pits and drift mines, and the coal in turn fed other industries such as iron mining and smelting, copper smelting, brick making, charcoal production and even an arsenic works. There were major limestone quarries along Gower's south coast, employing hundreds of people each, as well as silver mining in the Bishopston Valley. However, the greater part of Carmarthenshire and Gower continued to be dominated by traditional rural industries. After hard times during the 1840s, these became increasingly prosperous as the arrival of the railway opened up new markets.

By the 1920s, the region's extractive and manufacturing industries were in serious decline, and within a few decades most had ceased altogether. The scars of heavy industry have all but healed over, and the natural beauty of Wales's coastline is undeniable. Nevertheless, while walking the Wales Coast Path you will also be aware of how this is a landscape that has been shaped and moulded by thousands of years of human occupation.

Wildlife in **Carmarthen Bay** & **Gower**

Among the many pleasures of walking the **Wales Coast Path** are the regular encounters with wildlife. Day by day, you'll come across a wealth of animals and plants, both common and uncommon. The whole of the Gower Peninsula is an Area of Outstanding Natural Beauty, while both Carmarthen Bay and Burry Inlet have been designated Special Protection Areas for birds. The region's diverse and unspoilt habitats support a rich variety of wildlife, from Gower ponies, seabirds and orchids, to choughs, butterflies and Atlantic grey seals. Together, they add a whole new dimension to the walking experience.

Gower pony

Golden samphire

Sea holly	 *Silver-washed fritillary*
 *Atlantic grey seal*	 *Valerian*

Sea pinks, or 'thrift'

Chough

Wildfowl, waders & wild ponies

Carmarthen Bay and Gower's rich and varied marine habitats support a wealth of wildlife

One of the many pleasures of walking the Wales Coast Path is encountering the sheer wealth of seabirds, marine mammals, reptiles, wild flowers, butterflies and other wildlife along the way. At 870 miles long, the path passes through a range of diverse habitats and provides a vantage point to spot many interesting species, from rare birds and beautiful butterflies to playful seals or passing porpoises.

Roosting sanderling on the Loughor Estuary, Carmarthen Bay

The Carmarthen Bay and Gower section of the coast path is characterised by several distinct marine habitats — shallow silty seas, estuarine mudflats and rugged limestone cliffs — that together support a rich and varied mix of species. The importance of these habitats to wildlife is acknowledged in the range of statutory protections they enjoy. Both Carmarthen Bay and Burry Inlet (the seaward end of the River Loughor) have been designated Special Protection Areas for birds, while the whole of the Gower Peninsula has been designated an Area of Outstanding Natural Beauty (AONB). In specific areas, further protection is provided in the form of local nature reserves, Wildlife Trust Reserves and three National Nature Reserves — areas containing the very finest examples of our wildlife habitats.

Carmarthen Bay

The first few days' walking are dominated by the wide, shallow waters of Carmarthen Bay. The bay is of international importance because of its wintering population of common scoter, a species of large sea duck that feeds on crustaceans and molluscs. The bay's shallow, silty waters, typically less than ten metres in depth, are perfect for the bird, which needs to be able to dive to the seabed to seek its food. The bird was badly affected by the Sea Empress oil spill of 1996, but has since made a remarkable recovery – over 43,000 were recorded in Carmarthen Bay during the winter of 2010.

Burry Inlet, a large estuary between the Gower Peninsula and Carmarthenshire, is also a designated Special Protection Area. The estuary includes extensive areas of intertidal sand and mudflats, together with large sand dune systems where it joins the open sea. The site also contains the largest continuous area of salt marsh in Wales. The estuary supports large numbers of overwintering wildfowl and waders, which feed in the salt marshes and along the intertidal zone. There are also internationally significant populations of oystercatcher, shoveler and pintail, as well as large numbers of grazing Gower ponies.

Semi-wild Gower ponies on Landimore Marsh, Gower

Natural mimic: *Exotic bee orchids flourish on several of Gower's nature reserves*

Llanelli Wetland Centre

On the northern side of the estuary, between Llanelli and Loughor, is the Llanelli Wetland Centre, one of ten wetland nature reserves in the UK managed by the Wildfowl and Wetlands Trust. The reserve consists of 450 acres of lakes, pools, streams and lagoons along the shores of the Loughor Estuary – a diverse range of habitats attracting numerous plants and animals. One of its success stories has been to attract breeding pairs of little egrets, a species of small white heron almost extinct in Britain but now increasing in numbers. Other birds you may spot include lapwing, shelduck and warblers, and, on a winter's dusk, any of Britain's five native species of owl. During summer months, the reserve is also home to a range of non-avian forms of life, including rare species of butterfly, dragonfly and moth, water voles and even otters.

Gower Area of Outstanding Natural Beauty

The southern shore of the Loughor Estuary forms part of the Gower AONB. At the estuary's seaward end lies Whiteford National Nature Reserve, a low-lying peninsula that acts as a natural breakwater between the Loughor's muddy tidal waters and the open sea. The diverse array of habitats in the reserve is truly astonishing: dunes, beach, salt marsh, mudflats and woodland can all

Aerial acrobats: *Red-billed choughs have recently returned to Gower's sea cliffs*

be found within its 3,000 acres. In winter, wildfowl and waders are present in large numbers, while butterflies and blossoming wild flowers transform the dunes into a blaze of colour during spring and early summer. More than 250 species of wild flower have been recorded at Whiteford, making it one of the richest dune systems in the UK.

This abundance of wild flowers supports a rich variety of butterflies and other insects that rely on plant life for their survival. Specific butterfly species to look out for include the common blue, the small blue, the dark green fritillary and the grayling. The scarlet tiger moth, which in June and July can be seen flying during the day at Whiteford, is one of only a few species of moth to have evolved special mouth parts enabling it to feed on nectar. Another rare invertebrate found on the reserve is the narrow-mouthed whorl snail, a poorly understood animal that is believed to feed on the tiny fungal species found on decaying plant matter.

Choughs and peregrines

At the south-western end of the Gower Peninsula is the Gower Coast National Nature Reserve. The reserve comprises the spectacular tidal island of Worms Head and a line of limestone cliffs along the mainland coast. These are home to several species of grass and flower adapted to survive in strong winds and salt spray. With their mild, maritime climate, the south-facing cliffs are home to a number of species, such as the yellow whitlow grass, found nowhere else in Britain. The cliffs also attract large numbers of breeding seabirds, and in June and July the cliffs and sea are full of guillemots, razorbills and kittiwakes. Choughs and peregrine falcons also breed on the cliffs, while in the autumn Atlantic grey seal pups may be spotted on the rocky shore.

A few miles east is Oxwich National Nature Reserve — like Whiteford, another coastal area containing an impressively diverse range of habitats. Within a relatively small area can be found dunes, beach, woodland, salt marsh and freshwater marsh, all teeming with wildlife. Around 600 species of plant have been recorded here, including stinking helleborine, dune gentian, round-leaved wintergreen and rock whitebeam, along with rare species of invertebrate such as Cepero's groundhopper (*Tetrix ceperoi*), the hairy dragonfly and the ground beetle (*Nebria complanata*). A chalky substrate allows wild orchids to thrive, while lakes and reedbeds attract a wide array of birdlife. The reserve is home to a number of rare warblers and even the occasional bittern, while small numbers of wildfowl like teal and gadwall use the marshes as overwintering grounds.

Of course, the above is only a brief summary of the range of wildlife that may be encountered along this section of the Wales Coast Path. For further details about the region's natural heritage, check out the Natural Resources Wales website at **www.naturalresourceswales.gov.uk**

Two Atlantic grey seals stare inquisitively towards the shore

Day Sections

1. Tenby to Pendine *13 miles/ 20 kilometres*

2. Pendine to St Clears *11 miles/ 17 kilometres*

3. St Clears to Llansteffan *10 miles/ 16 kilometres*

4. Llansteffan to Carmarthen *9 miles/ 15 kilometres*

5. Carmarthen to Kidwelly *14 miles/ 22 kilometres*

6. Kidwelly to Burry Port *10 miles/ 17 kilometres*

7. Burry Port to Loughor *11 miles/ 17 kilometres*

8. Loughor to Llanmadoc *13 miles/ 21 kilometres*

9. Llanmadoc to Rhossili *10 miles/ 17 kilometres*

10. Rhossili to Oxwich *12 miles/ 19 kilometres*

11. Oxwich to Caswell Bay *9 miles/ 14 kilometres*

12. Caswell Bay to Swansea Marina *9 miles/ 15 kilometres*

The Carmarthen Bay & Gower
section of the
Wales Coast Path

Tenby to Pendine

Distance: *13 miles/ 20 kilometres* | **Start:** *South Beach, Tenby SN 134 002*
Finish: *Pendine SN 233 079* | **Maps:** *Ordnance Survey Explorer 177 and OL36, Landranger 158*

Outline: A varied section comprising south Pembrokeshire's coastal resorts and the rugged, undulating coastline of west Carmarthenshire.

The first half of this section passes through the popular tourist area of south Pembrokeshire. In between the busy resorts of Tenby, Saundersfoot and Amroth the path passes across wooded cliffs and along a former tramway. The second half of the walk, between Amroth and Pendine, is the more demanding, with numerous steep climbs and descents and no on-route facilities. The pay-off is the rugged beauty of the coast: wild, unspoilt and uninhabited save for the occasional farm. A dramatic vista along the length of Pendine Sands concludes a fabulous introduction to the Carmarthenshire coast.

Services: *Tenby is a large seaside resort with lots of accommodation, banks, post offices, shops, pubs and bars, restaurants, cafés and takeaways. More pubs, cafés and toilets can be found on route in Saundersfoot, Wiseman's Bridge and Amroth. Tenby Taxis: 01834 843678*

Don't miss: St Mary's Church, Tenby – one of the largest parish churches in Wales | **Saundersfoot Harbour** – attractive marina in a historic industrial port | **Gilman Point** – a fabulous view along the length of Pendine Sands

▲ *The view down the beach at Amroth*

Tenby

There are few Welsh seaside resorts as historically interesting as Tenby. The town has largely retained its medieval street pattern, which forms a maze of narrow lanes and alleyways inside the old town wall (built by Anglo-Norman settlers to protect the town from Welsh raids). Particularly worth a look are Five Arches Gate and St Mary's Church, one of the largest and most extravagant parish churches in Wales. From a slightly later date is the Tudor Merchant's House, a late fifteenth-century town house that would have belonged to a prosperous merchant.

Most houses in Tenby, however, are of Georgian construction, dating from a time when the town was enjoying a boom as a fashionable seaside resort. A key figure was William Paxton, who founded a bathhouse in 1805 in which visiting patrons could experience the curative properties of salt water under cover. The houses that sprung up during this period tended to follow the town's historic layout, creating a delightful higgledy-piggledy effect. As you wander the streets you'll be constantly surprised by an unexpected view of one of Tenby's two beaches or of Caldey Island or St Catherine's Island. This is without doubt a fabulous place to start a section of the Wales Coast Path.

Pastel-hued Georgian houses surround Tenby harbour

Harbour mirror: *Tenby's colourful houses are reflected in the harbour at low tide*

The route: **Tenby to Pendine**

1 A walkway and set of steps leads up from Tenby's **South Beach Bar Grill** to the **Esplanade**, and it's from the top of this steep ascent from South Beach that the route begins.

Turn right and walk along the Esplanade to Tenby's **old town wall**. Follow the road left, but then go through the arch on the right. Swing right to continue along the **seafront**. Ignore the steps down into the **harbour**; instead swing left with the road. Take the narrow lane on the right and then turn left along the **High Street**, passing 👁 **St Mary's Church**, on the left.

Beyond the shops and restaurants, the road passes above North Beach. Take the next road on the right — The Croft. As the road swings up into a cul-de-sac, take the lane on the left, soon picking up a roadside path on the right. Where the lane ends, close to the entrance of Meadow Farm, you'll see two paths continuing ahead. Take the one on the right, soon climbing concrete steps. At a path junction close to **Waterwynch Beach**, turn left.

2 Dropping to a lane, take the path opposite — through the trees. This is the first of several areas of **Hean Castle Estate woodland** passed between

here and Saundersfoot. After the bridge, bear right. Emerging briefly from the trees via a gate, keep to the path at the base of the slope and then head along another, shorter woodland trail. Walk with a fence on the right over **Rowston Hill**, but after that you're back out on the cliff again.

There are some good views back to Tenby from time to time, but it is to the next section of coast, the final few kilometres of the Pembrokeshire Coast Path, that your gaze will inevitably be drawn — when the thick vegetation

An island fortress

Dominating the small tidal island of St Catherine's in Tenby is a 'Palmerston fort'. Named after the prime minister Lord Palmerston, a powerful advocate of their construction, these forts were built in important strategic positions along the British coast in response to a perceived French naval threat during the 1860s. This never materialised and St Catherine's Fort was finally abandoned by the military after World War Two.

Summer breeze: *On the cliffs above Monkstone Beach and Monkstone Point*

allows. Those views improve considerably after the long, steep climb out of **Lodge Valley** and up to the gate near the Coastguard lookout at **Monkstone**. Cross the track here and continue following the fence on your right.

Before long, you reach a junction of paths in another area of **Hean Castle Estate woodland**. Go straight across, descending steeply at first. Turn left at a junction after a small bridge. The path climbs uphill briefly before winding downhill, past the fenced adit of a disused iron ore mine, to a junction above a beach. You'll see two paths heading uphill on the other side. Take the one on the right and, when this forks, bear right. Climbing again, keep right. Finally, leave the Hean Castle Estate woods, and drop to the road.

3 Turn right and follow the road up to a T-junction with the **B4316**, along which you turn right. Follow the road down into **Saundersfoot**, a popular little resort. Don't miss picturesque 👁 **Saundersfoot Harbour.** Turn right at a mini-roundabout — into the car park — and go left, beyond the buildings. Keep straight ahead, along **The Strand**. At the far end of this road, a path leads into the **first of three tunnels**, this one lit.

The Saundersfoot area represents yet another change in the underlying ge-ology along the Pembrokeshire Coast Path, and this tunnel is evidence of that. With the two tunnels further north, it formed part of the Saundersfoot Railway, which connected the mines and ironworks at Stepaside and Kilgetty with the harbour at Saundersfoot.

The coal measures here represent the youngest rocks along the coast, formed as the sea levels fell towards the end of the Carboniferous period, leaving vast areas of swamp. Coal had been dug in the area for several centuries, but it was only in the nineteenth century that mining and its associated industries really took off. Nearby deposits of haematite and reserves of limestone led to the rise of smelting and iron-working. The harbour at Saundersfoot flourished, and, by 1837, it had five jetties handling coal, iron ore, pig iron and brick, exporting to places as far away as Hong Kong.

On the other side of this first tunnel, keep left, along the walkway and across the car park entrance at **Coppet Hall Point**. On your right, looking out over the beach, is a new restaurant, café, toilets, and an outdoor activity centre. Swing right at the far end of the development, soon going through another, shorter tunnel.

The interesting, sloping rock formations on this beach were created by the

Saundersfoot Harbour is rightly popular with visitors

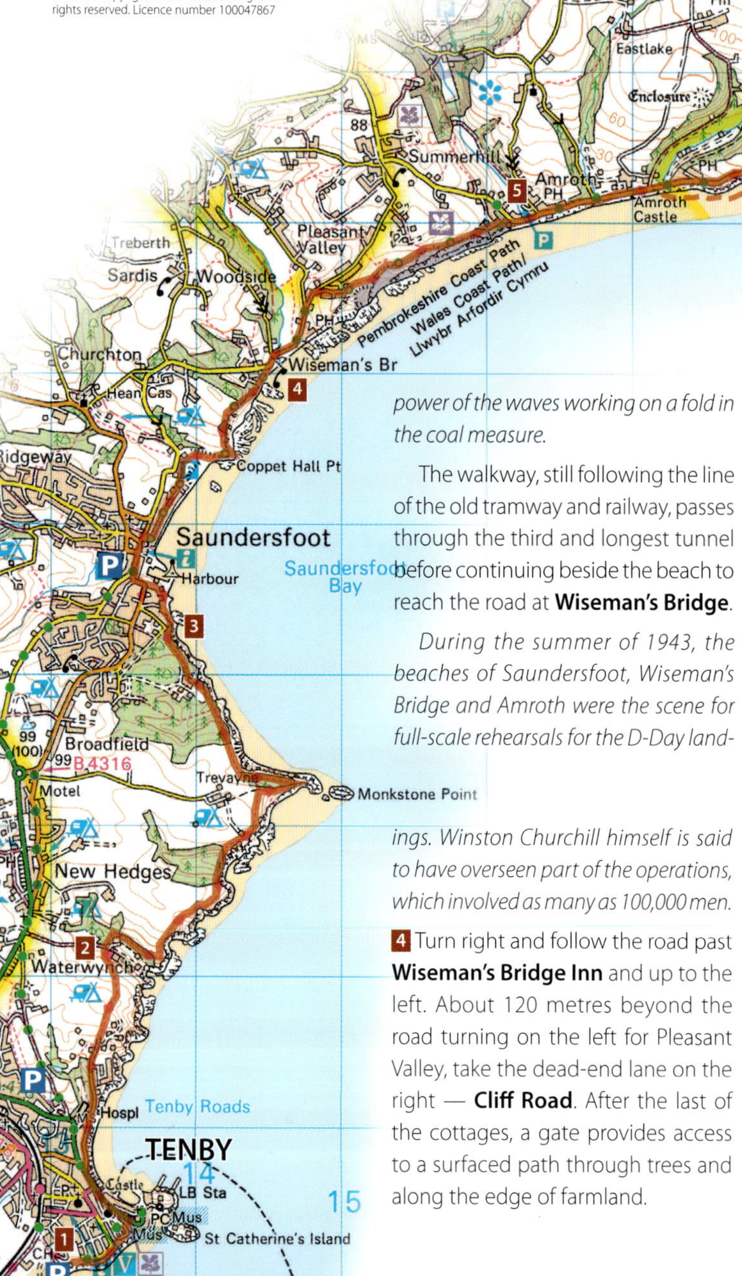

power of the waves working on a fold in the coal measure.

The walkway, still following the line of the old tramway and railway, passes through the third and longest tunnel before continuing beside the beach to reach the road at **Wiseman's Bridge**.

During the summer of 1943, the beaches of Saundersfoot, Wiseman's Bridge and Amroth were the scene for full-scale rehearsals for the D-Day land-ings. Winston Churchill himself is said to have overseen part of the operations, which involved as many as 100,000 men.

4 Turn right and follow the road past **Wiseman's Bridge Inn** and up to the left. About 120 metres beyond the road turning on the left for Pleasant Valley, take the dead-end lane on the right — **Cliff Road**. After the last of the cottages, a gate provides access to a surfaced path through trees and along the edge of farmland.

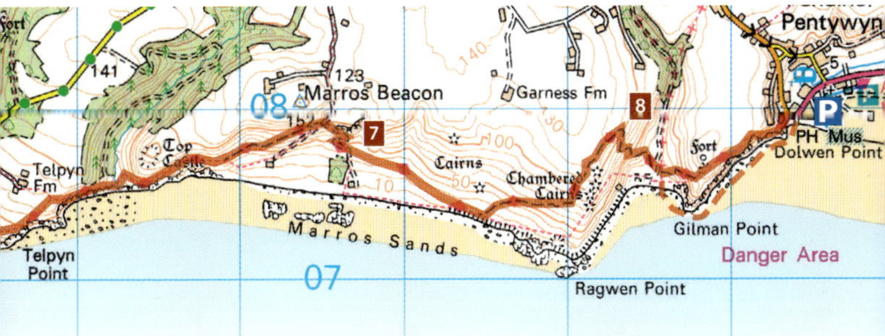

Watch for a gate on the right with coast path waymarkers on it. Go through this and turn left. The grassy path provides a welcome relief after all those kilometres of asphalt and concrete. Later, go left in the woods to descend the steps to the road at **Amroth**. You're nearly there now!

5 Turn right along the road. *At low tide, watch for tree stumps on the beach, the remains of an ancient woodland, long submerged by the sea.* After about 1km of roadside walking, passing the gateway to **Amroth Castle** on the way, you reach the boundary of the **Pembrokeshire Coast National Park**. *Plaques next to the bridge and a sign pointing back to St Dogmael's, 300 kilometres away, herald your achievement in reaching the end of the* **Pembrokeshire Coast Path National Trail**.

From **The New Inn** in **Amroth**, either follow the minor road up the hill or, if the tide is out, avoid this initial road section by walking along the beach.

Alternative route: *A short stroll along the beach*

Walk along the sand as far as SN 182 073 — about 300 metres to the north-west of **Telpyn Point** — where a short section of gravel path climbs back up to the official route. (It's theoretically possible at low tide to walk all the way to Pendine along the beach, but you would need to get your timings spot-on to achieve this.)

If following the **official route** from Amroth, continue up the road as far as a house called '**Merrifield**' on the right. *Looking back as you climb, there are great views around the curve of Carmarthen Bay towards Saundersfoot, Tenby and Caldey Island.* A footpath to the left of 'Merrifield 'winds its way along the cliff tops between the road and the sea, before descending steeply down steps to a cross-path. The alternative low tide route rejoins the official path here from the right.

6 Keep ahead, down further steps, to a **wooden footbridge**. Cross a tiny stream marking the border between Pembrokeshire and Carmarthenshire and follow the signed path as it bears slightly right. The path climbs steadily through gorse, offering fine views ahead towards the Gower Peninsula. After the path levels out, you will find yourself looking down the long, straight beach of Marros Sands (covered at high tide). The undulating path to **Ragwen Point** at the far end of the beach is much longer and tougher than it appears.

A zigzagging descent leads down to a footbridge in a wooded valley. This is the lower end of **Teague's Wood**, *where local legend claims the last wild wolf in Wales was killed*. More zigzags take you back up the cliffs and below the Iron Age fortress of **Top Castle**. The path continues to climb, passing high above Marros Sands before descending again. At the bottom of the slope, follow the arrow directing you left.

Climb again, passing a bench on the left near the top of the slope. After a short level section, there is a further climb, this time rewarded by two benches! Cross an access track to 'Underhill' and continue on a rougher vehicle track, which soon starts to descend. Follow the track round a sharp right-hand bend (so you are now heading the wrong way along the coast) and then back around a sharp left-hand bend. As it starts to turn right again, in the direction of the sea, leave the track through a metal kissing gate on the left.

Fossilised tree stumps on Amroth beach

Rock and sand: *Looking down into Morfa Bychan bay with Gilman Point and Pendine Sands behind*

Detour: *To Marros village, church and campsite*
A left turn along the vehicle track will take you inland to the hamlet of **Marros**. There is a fine church here, a campsite, and an unusual war memorial inspired by the Neolithic burial chambers above Ragwen Point.

7 The **official route** remains enclosed by trees and scrub for some distance, obscuring views towards the sea. Cross a stream by a wooden stile and gate and then a private track running down to **Marros Sands**. After passing through a metal gate, the coastal views open out once more. Ignore a path leading down to a stile on the right, instead keeping ahead on a higher path alongside a fence. The Path continues across the coastal slope, joining a section of **boardwalk** over marshy ground. Parts of the Coast Path beyond the boardwalk are much eroded and may be muddy after wet weather.

As you approach the end of Marros Sands, begin to climb steadily up the headland above **Ragwen Point**, eventually bearing left, away from the sea, to ascend more steeply. *Located to the right of the path are a number of* **Neolithic burial chambers**, *though the jumble of slabs, gorse and bracken makes these difficult to identify.*

Long and flat: *The vast expanse of Pendine Sands and Pendine Burrows seen from Gilman Point*

Go through a kissing gate and shortly meet a grassy track at the top of the climb. After turning right along the track, you will catch your first glimpse of Pendine Sands.

8 As the track begins to descend, turn right onto a narrower path. A long descent leads to the small bay of **Morfa Bychan** (not named on OS maps). Follow the path along the seaward side of a battered slab of concrete to a kissing gate leading onto a track.

This concrete slab was part of a World War Two training exercise called 'Exercise Jantzen' in which troops practised storming Morfa Bychan from the sea in preparation for the Normandy landings. Other evidence of this exercise are pyramid-shaped tank-busting blocks — so-called 'dragon's teeth' — embedded in the sand of the beach.

Alternative route: *Along the beach*

At low tide, you may prefer to avoid the steep climb over Gilman Point by walking around to **Pendine** along the beach.

If following the **official route**, cross the track to a path ahead (signed to 'Pendine') and climb steeply. Note the remnants of **Iron Age earthworks** at the top of the climb and continue ahead to enjoy amazing views from the end of 👁 **Gilman Point** along the length of Pendine Sands.

Follow the path along the cliffs above the beach and start your descent to **Pendine**. A long flight of steps will deposit you on a concrete walkway. Continue ahead past a number of cafés and gift shops to the corner of a main road. **The Springwell Inn** is to your left, while a short distance along the main road ahead are bus stops and a car park.

Sheer cliffs and sea ducks

The rocky headlands of Telpyn Point and Gilman Point, on the high cliffs between Amroth and Pendine, contain the largest colonies of sea birds in Carmarthenshire. The cliffs are an important wintering ground for the common scoter, a species of sea duck that feeds on crustaceans and molluscs. They were badly affected by the Sea Empress oil spill of 1996, but have since made a remarkable recovery — more than 43,000 were recorded in Carmarthen Bay in winter 2010.

Pendine to St Clears

Distance: *11 miles / 17 kilometres* | **Start:** *Pendine SN 233 079*
Finish: *St Clears SN 281 153* | **Maps:** *Ordnance Survey Explorer 177, Landranger 158 & 159*

Outline: A mixed bag of a section: mainly inland field paths, but also some fine walking along the Tâf Estuary near Laugharne.

An MOD firing range occupies Pendine Burrows, forcing the Wales Coast Path to detour inland for much of the way to Laugharne. An optional detour along Pendine Sands heads towards Ginst Point where there are fine estuary views across the Tâf (please note: there is currently no legal right of way or permissive route linking Ginst Point to Laugharne). You may also like to explore the quirky little town of Laugharne. The final section to St Clears consists mainly of tracks and field paths through farmland.

Services: *There are pubs, takeaways, toilets and shops in both Pendine and Laugharne. The latter has a wide range of places in which to eat or drink, as well as a cash point and a pharmacy. Carmarthen TIC: 01267 231557 | carmarthentic@ carmarthenshire.gov.uk.*

👁 **Don't miss:** **Museum, Pendine** – museum exploring Pendine's history as a site for land speed record attempts | **Laugharne Castle** – a magnificent medieval fortress turned Tudor mansion | **Dylan Thomas Boathouse, Laugharne** – home to the Welsh poet for the last four years of his life

▲ *Laugharne Castle and tidal saltmarshes from the air*

Pendine

Historically, Pendine was divided into two parts: an old hilltop settlement around the parish church and a coastal harbour settlement above the beach. The coastal part of the village expanded significantly after the eighteenth century, when Pendine evolved into a small but thriving seaside resort.

It was not just tourists who were attracted to Pendine. During the 1920s, the village's 10 kilometres of hard, flat sands helped it to achieve lasting fame as a site for land speed record attempts. Malcolm Campbell became the first man to break the 150mph barrier in July 1925 and in February 1927 set a new record of 174mph. Only weeks later, Welsh driver J. G. Parry-Thomas died in an attempt to retake the record from Campbell when his car 'Babs' overturned. Babs was buried in nearby sand dunes but was later removed and restored. The car is now on display in the village's Museum of Speed.

Another record breaker associated with Pendine is English aviator Amy Johnson, who began a nonstop transatlantic flight to America from Pendine Sands in 1933. During the Second World War, the beach was acquired by the Ministry of Defence and used as a firing range. Regular weapons testing continues to this day, leading to restrictions on public access.

Pendine Sands stretch into the distance for more than six miles

The route: **Pendine to St Clears**

1 From the **Spring Well Inn** in **Pendine**, keep ahead along the main road for a short distance, then bear right behind the **Beach Hotel.** Follow a walkway past a beach café towards the 👁 **Museum of Speed** and turn left through a car park (passing public toilets) back towards the main road.

Detour: *An out and back exploration of Pendine Sands*
Because of the existence of an MOD weapons testing range behind Pendine Sands, the Wales Coast Path is forced to follow an inland route between Pendine and Laugharne, mainly alongside the A4066. However, when the weapons range is not in use (most weekends), it is worth taking a stroll along the hard, flat sands of the beach, which stretch for over 6 miles (10 km) as far as Ginst Point. (A red flag flying at the Pendine end of the beach indicates that weapons testing is taking place and you should not proceed farther.)

Pendine Sands is most famous as a site for early land speed record attempts (see introduction to section), but the quieter, eastern end of the beach towards Ginst Point has an equally well-deserved reputation among birdwatchers. Near the mouth of the River Taf, the intertidal sands are particularly rich in invertebrates, attracting a wide range of feeding gulls and waders. Sea buckthorn in the extensive scrub behind the beach attracts finches and other passerines (songbirds), while the marshy fields behind the dunes are used by large flocks of golden plover and lapwing.

Turn right as you leave the car park and follow the pavement alongside the A4066. As you leave Pendine, continue onto a wide tarmac cycle path that follows the road as far as **Llanmiloe**. Cross a

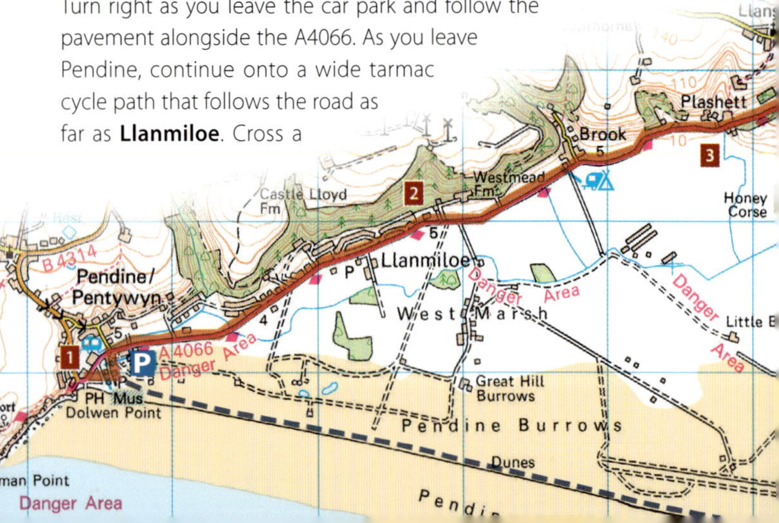

parking area near playing fields into a playground and keep ahead to pass **Llanmiloe Post Office**. Shortly, bear left across the main road to a parallel residential road on the far side.

2 Rejoin the main road by a bus shelter and continue along the pavement to a second bus shelter. Cross the road to a kissing gate and continue on an enclosed field path parallel to the main road.

The path returns to the main road for a short distance near an access road to the firing range. Follow the grass verge until just past the turn-off, where a kissing gate leads back to a parallel field path. Follow fields adjacent to the **A4066** as far as **Plashett,** where you must once more return to the road itself. (Before reaching Plashett, don't bear right onto a track; this takes you away from the main road on the wrong side of a field boundary. The correct route crosses the track to a stile and continues to the immediate right of the main road.)

Sea fortress: *Now a ruin, Laugharne Castle once guarded the strategic entrance to the Tâf estuary*

3 Follow the roadside verge for close to one kilometre. Shortly after cresting the brow of a hill, take the road on the right signed to 'Hurst House Hotel'. As you walk down the hill you will be able to see the sea for the first time since leaving Pendine. Just past a bungalow at the bottom of the slope (opposite the entrance to **Coygen Quarry**), turn left along a track leading to **Salt House Farm**.

As you approach the farm, fork right to bypass the buildings. Continue along the track, which ends at a kissing gate near the **River Tâf.** Climb steeply through woodland on a narrow path.

At the top of the hill is an **information board** where the trees have been cleared to create a fantastic viewpoint across the estuary. *On a fine day, you should be able to see across Carmarthen Bay to Pembrey Forest and the Gower Peninsula.* A level path continues through woodland before descending to a tarmac track on the edge of Laugharne. Turn left towards a large car park below 👁 **Laugharne Castle.**

4 From the car park in **Laugharne**, take the tarmac path below the castle signed to 'Dylan Thomas' Boathouse', then follow another sign directing you left uphill.

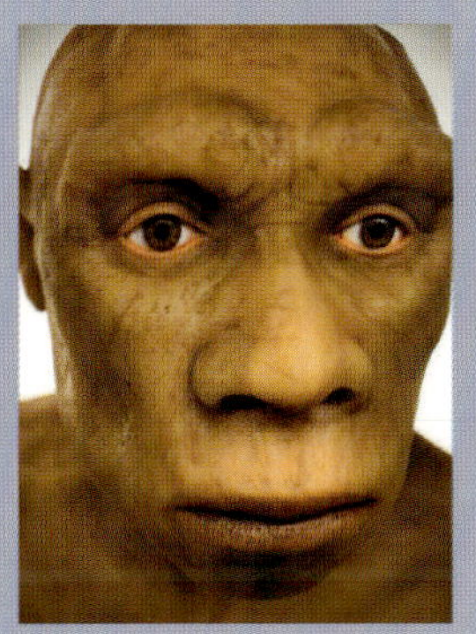

Alternative route: *Walkway above the estuary*

It is also possible to continue along the walkway above the estuary
and take the next flight of steps on the left. These are signed to the
'Boathouse' and emerge on the lane near Thomas's 'writing shed'.

For the **official route**, bear right along a narrow street, then right again at a
T-junction. A little farther on, another right turn, onto a dead-end lane, leads
down to a narrow road above the estuary. Continue past **Dylan Thomas's**

Coygen's cavemen

*Before quarrying began here, an extensive
cave system ran deep into the limestone. Stone
tools discovered in the cave show it was being
used by Neanderthal people between 60,000
and 40,000 years ago, and bones from Ice Age
animals, including hyenas, were also found. By
around 30,000 years ago, Neanderthals, who had
dominated Ice Age Europe for more than 100,000
years, had become extinct and been replaced by
anatomically modern humans.*

Dylan Thomas's favourite bar, Laugharne

Dylan Thomas's 'New Walk'

Tracing the inspiration for 'Poem in October'

Between Salt House Farm and Laugharne, the Wales Coast Path crosses a steep, wooded shoulder of land on the eastern edge of Sir John's Hill. The path, which runs high above the River Tâf's estuary, is known locally as the 'New Walk' and was constructed by Laugharne's town corporation in 1856 to provide access to valuable cockle beds on the marshes. Prior to this, the only access to the beds had been via a cart track across the tidal mud flats below Sir John's Hill. This was flooded twice a day at high tide, preventing passage to and from the beds.

During the 1940s, the path became one of Dylan Thomas's favourite Laugharne walks; his well-known landscape poem, 'Poem in October', describes an ascent of Sir John's Hill on the poet's 'thirtieth year to heaven'. This section of Coast Path is now part of a short waymarked trail — 'Dylan's Birthday Walk' — tracing the inspiration behind 'Poem in October'.

If celebrating your birthday, you can claim a range of complimentary gifts from participating businesses in Laugharne (including a free pint in Brown's Hotel) by reciting the poem's final lines ('O may my heart's truth…') and producing evidence of your birth date!

More information: 'Poem in October', Collected Poems: Dylan Thomas (Everyman, 2003). www. dylanthomasbirthdaywalk.co.uk

Poet's perch: *Dylan Thomas's Boathouse overlooks the broad Tâf estuary*

'writing shed' and then the 👁 **Boathouse** itself (access to the latter is down steps on the right) *It was in this house, now a museum, that Thomas spent the last four years of his life, between 1949 and 1953.*

At the end of the lane, keep ahead onto a gravel track across the wooded slopes above the estuary. Cross a road and continue through more woodland until you emerge in a field. The path now follows the curve of the estuary left as far as the beautiful gardens of **Delacorse**. Go through the yard of the house and start a long, steady climb along a tree-enclosed track.

5 At the top of the hill, turn sharply right onto a tarmac lane to 'Brixtarw'. Continue past the **farm** onto a grassy track, shortly joining a gravel track in woodland. Do not go through the next gate ahead, but turn left onto a narrow path. This descends through trees to the **River Tâf** and continues to the left along the bottom edge of fields.

At the end of the third field, go through a kissing gate onto a short section of **boardwalk** below trees. The path bears left, away from the river, and emerges from the trees near the top edge of a large field. Follow the field boundary right and then left, as it curves towards the main road. As you approach the road, bear right so as to continue along the edge of the field with the road on the other side of the hedge to your left.

Medieval Laugharne

Quirky town where medieval customs flourish

The Normans founded a castle at Laugharne in the early twelfth century, an earth and timber defence attacked and destroyed by the Welsh on a number of occasions. In the 1260s, Norman strongman Guy de Brian IV began constructing a much stronger masonry castle. This was extended and embellished by subseqent generations of de Brians, until the death of Guy de Brian VII in 1390 led to a long period of decline.

It was Sir John Perrot who revived the castle's fortunes, converting it into a substantial Tudor mansion in the late sixteenth century. Original features, such as the towering ramparts with their mock battlements, were retained and even embellished by Perrot for ornamental effect. Un-

View from Laugharne Castle

fortunately, they failed to withstand a Roundhead assault during the Civil War and the mansion was subsequently abandoned. After several centuries of neglect, it was eventually incorporated into the grounds of Castle House; formal gardens were laid in the outer ward and a gazebo built on the ramparts above the estuary. This splendid little summer house was used as a writing room by both Dylan Thomas and Richard Hughes during the 1930s.

The history of Laugharne town is as old and fascinating as its castle. The town's charter was established by the de Brians, who founded Laugharne Corporation in 1291 and granted its burgesses – who were mainly English – with a range of special privileges to ensure their loyalty against the Welsh. The tactic worked: although only a few miles from areas where the everyday language was Welsh, Laugharne has always been an English-speaking town, with customs and traditions that set it apart from the rest of Carmarthenshire.

At the centre of this distinct identity is Laugharne's unique corporation – the last medieval corporation left in the UK. As well as managing the town's affairs, the corporation

Laugharne Town Hall

> ***"I am spending Whitsun in the strangest town in Wales... "***
>
> *Dylan Thomas, letter to Pamela Hansford Johnson, May 1934*

is also responsible for maintaining more colourful traditions, such as the Laugharne Common Walk. Led by the Portreeve (the leader of the corporation, appointed annually), this all-day walk is a variation on the medieval tradition of 'beating the bounds', retracing and thereby reaffirming the town's ancient boundaries. Along the route, there are numerous stops for bread, cheese and ale, and at each key boundary stone a youngster is required to provide its correct name. A wrong answer results in the victim (usually a young lady) being hoisted upside down and cermonially beaten three times on the bottom!

More information: Laugharne's official website at www.laugharne.info is a good starting point for anyone wanting to find out more about the town.

River song: *Beyond Dylan Thomas's Boathouse, the Tâf curves inland towards St Clears*

Drop to a **footbridge** and kissing gate near a pond. In the next field, bear right towards a lone tree below electricity wires. Continue past the tree to a kissing gate in the bottom corner of the field, then follow the field edge directly ahead. As you approach the **river** once more, ignore stiles to the right, instead staying with the field edge as it curves to the left. Climb away from the river, then join an enclosed path between fences back to the main road. This turns right and continues parallel to the road.

6 Rejoin the main road and continue for a short distance along the grassy verge. Just before a left-hand bend, cross to a waymark post and join a path that cuts through the undergrowth above a dangerous corner. Drop back to the road, then look for a kissing gate a short distance ahead along the left-hand verge. This provides access to another parallel path, which follows the **A4066** north as far as a junction with a minor road. Cross to the pavement on the far side and continue towards St Clears.

After hurrying across a **narrow bridge** over the **Tâf**, turn immediately right onto a narrow road to the left of 'Manordaf' B&B. This curves left past **St Clears Boating Club** and then right to a bridge over **Afon Cynin** and the end of the section.

To continue into the centre of **St Clears**, bear left before the bridge onto a path past a pumping station. Keep ahead onto a residential road, then ahead again onto a track past an industrial unit. With the church ahead, bear right onto a signed cycle path. A pleasant stroll along the banks of the **Cynin** leads to an underpass below the busy A40. Emerge in a car park in the centre of **St Clears**, with toilets, bus stops and other facilities close by.

Ferries and causeways

The Tâf and Towy estuaries have hampered travel around Carmarthen Bay for centuries. Two small sailing ferries — one crossing the Tâf from Laugharne, the other connecting Llansteffan and Ferryside across the Towy — connected Carmarthenshire's coastal settlements until the 1950s. On the shallower Tâf, another solution was to ford the river at low tide: medieval causeways are visible near Delacorse. Today, the ferries between Ferryside and Llansteffan are running again.
www.carmarthenbayferries.co.uk/timetable

St Clears to Llansteffan

Distance: *10 miles / 16 kilometres* | **Start:** *St Clears SN 281 153* |
Finish: *Llansteffan SN 352 104* | **Maps:** *Ordnance Survey Explorer 177,
Landranger 158 & 159*

Outline: Another section running mainly through farmland, though concluding with some dramatic coastal views from Wharley Point.

From St Clears, the Wales Coast Path follows mainly field paths and quiet country lanes back down the Tâf Valley. There are no great views, but historical interest is provided by the ruins of two former churches (St Michael's and St Teilo's) on the medieval pilgrim route to St David's. After returning to the coast at Wharley Point, there is a breathtaking view across the Tâf and Towy estuaries. The winding clifftop path between here and Llansteffan is the most rewarding stretch of the day.

Services: *There's a wide range of services in the small town of St Clears, including pubs, takeaways, toilets, shops, a post office and a bank, as well as B&B accommodation and a Travelodge hotel. Carmarthen TIC: 01267 231557 | carmarthentic@ carmarthenshire.gov.uk.*

Don't miss: St Michael's Church – former parish church on the pilgrim route to St David's | **Wharley Point** – stunning views across Carmarthenshire's 'Three Rivers' | **St Anthony's Well** – holy well associated with an early Welsh saint

▲ *The 'West Wales Centre for Arts and Crafts', St Clears*

St Clears

Like many Welsh towns, **St Clears** is Norman in origin. The Normans had penetrated the area by the end of the eleventh century and established a motte-and-bailey castle on the junction of the Tâf and Cynin rivers. Nearby, they founded a Cluniac priory, which later became the town's parish church. The present church building still contains a Romanesque arch dating from the twelfth century and has some of the best surviving examples of Norman carved work in Carmarthenshire.

By the twelfth century, the settlement that had developed outside the castle gates had grown into a small town and was the administrative centre of a Norman colony. The Norman hold over St Clears was tenuous, however, and both town and castle frequently fell into the hands of the Welsh. The failure to establish English settlement on a permanent basis enabled the Welsh language to re-establish itself in the town, creating a sharp cultural and linguistic divide between St Clears and neighbouring Laugharne.

After centuries of peace, St Clears was again the scene of violent disturbances during the Rebecca Riots of 1839–43, when tollgates throughout West Wales were attacked and destroyed by farmers and agricultural workers dressed as women.

Wooden sculpture in St Clears commemorating the Rebecca Riots

Lost church: *Parishioners once reached remote St Michael's Church by boat*

The route: **St Clears to Llansteffan**

1 Cross the **Afon Cynin** just upstream from **St Clears Boating Club** and keep ahead on a concrete track. Where the track swings right towards sewage works, bear slightly left to a foot gate and stone stile. Cross into a field and bear right towards the far corner, aiming for a house on the brow of the hill.

Go through a foot gate in the top right-hand corner of the field and join a grassy track which swings left, joining a wider track rising from a stone barn on the right. Bear left through another foot gate and climb to a junction with a gravel track by a barn. Follow the track right to a left-hand bend, then fork right through a gate onto a smaller track. This descends, swings right, then continues as a grassy track along the edge of a field.

The track becomes undefined, but continue along the edge of the field to two kissing gates. Go through and bear half left down a large field towards a lone tree in the far corner. In the next field, aim to the left of a pylon, crossing a farm track, and continue to a kissing gate onto a lane.

Detour: *To St Michael's Church*

To visit the atmospheric ruins of 👁 **St Michael's Church**, turn right at the first lane and follow it to a group of houses known as **Trefenty**. Turn left behind farm buildings, then bear right across a field in the

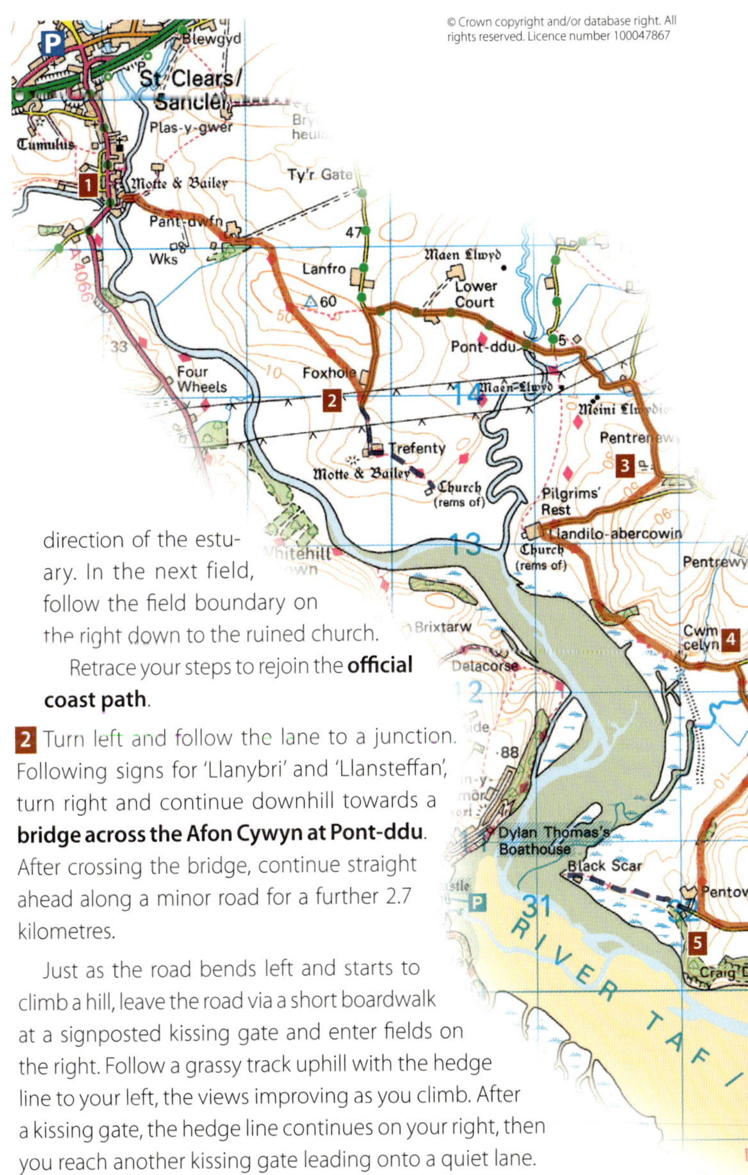

direction of the estuary. In the next field, follow the field boundary on the right down to the ruined church.

Retrace your steps to rejoin the **official coast path**.

2 Turn left and follow the lane to a junction. Following signs for 'Llanybri' and 'Llansteffan', turn right and continue downhill towards a **bridge across the Afon Cywyn at Pont-ddu**. After crossing the bridge, continue straight ahead along a minor road for a further 2.7 kilometres.

Just as the road bends left and starts to climb a hill, leave the road via a short boardwalk at a signposted kissing gate and enter fields on the right. Follow a grassy track uphill with the hedge line to your left, the views improving as you climb. After a kissing gate, the hedge line continues on your right, then you reach another kissing gate leading onto a quiet lane.

3 Turn right and follow the lane downhill to a farm. *There are further ruins behind the farm belonging to* **St Teilo's Church**. Turn left onto a track in front

Sense of space: *Panoramic view across the Tâf estuary to Pendine Burrows from Pentowyn*

of the farm buildings. Bear right to a double set of field gates and follow an enclosed concrete track to the left. Where this becomes a grassy track swinging uphill to the left, keep ahead into a field, aiming for the bottom edge of a wooded area above the **Tâf Estuary**.

Follow a track through the trees close to the estuary. On leaving the wood, drop right, heading downhill across a field to a foot gate, and bear left along the edge of the **salt marsh** in the direction of **Cwm-celyn farm**. Ignore a track climbing left and continue along the edge of the open marsh to a gate into the **farmyard**. Continue through and join a lane ahead.

4 Turn right where you meet a lane at a corner. After about 700 metres, as the lane starts to climb, turn right opposite a house on the left. Immediately bear left into a field and cut across the field corner to a stile ahead. Turn left through two fields, then pass through a rough section below a steep wooded slope. Bear right, then left below trees, and continue onto a grassy path climbing to the left between ferns. *As you climb, views open out towards Laugharne and across Carmarthen Bay to Caldey Island.*

After a gate/stile, the path bears right and descends through trees. Emerge

by a fence to the left of a house and follow it down to a kissing gate and onto a lane.

*This quiet country lane was one of the major highways of medieval Wales. Known as '**The King's Way**', it connected south and west Wales via two ferry crossings on the rivers Tâf and Towy. The road remained an important highway until the eighteenth century, when the development of better quality turnpike roads led to quicker, more direct routes across Wales.*

Saint David's pilgrim route

St Michael's was the parish church for Llanfihangel Abercywyn until 1848, when a new church was built beside the A40. The original building lay along the pilgrim route to St David's; tradition says that six medieval gravestones here belong to pilgrims who died mid-journey. Nearby is the junction of the Tâf and Cywyn rivers. It was customary for pilgrims to cross the latter from St Teilo's Church on the opposite bank — an adjacent farmhouse is still known as Pilgrims' Rest.

Time and tide: *The mouth of the River Towy seen from the wooded path below Wharley Point*

Detour: *To the former ferry crossing at Black Scar*

To visit the former ferry crossing at Black Scar Point, turn right down the lane, keeping straight ahead past a farm entrance on the left and a track to Pentowyn on the right. Passing the lane to 'Pond Cottage', continue ahead on to an unsurfaced road, eventually reaching a metal farm gate. Go through this and down a grassy path, ignoring any gates to your left. The path – which can be muddy – ends at a wooden stile and gate directly opposite Dylan Thomas' Boathouse. There are also excellent views of the rest of Laugharne, including of the castle and Sir John's Hill.

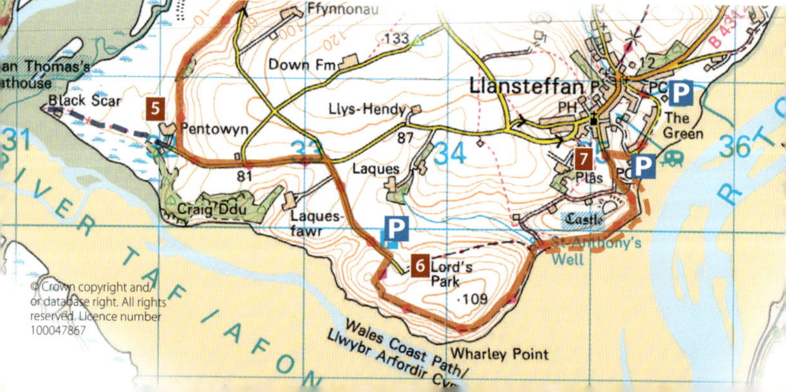

5 For the **official route**, turn left up the hill and climb steeply. *As the road levels out, the open sea becomes visible for the first time on this section, and there is a clear view across the bay to the Gower Peninsula and the tapering point of Worms Head.* Take the next road on the right, signed **'Lord's Park Farm'**.

As you approach the farm — *where there are views towards Llansteffan Castle and Ferryside through a gap in the hills to the left* — turn right through a National Trust gate onto an enclosed grassy path signed to 'Wharley Point'. This crests the brow of a hill and drops gently towards the sea. Shortly curve left along the high cliffs of 👁 **Wharley Point.**

This splendid viewpoint overlooks the confluence of the Tâf, Towy and Gwendraeth rivers as they merge in the shallow, shimmering waters of Carmarthen Bay. There is no better place to appreciate the full extent of the bay, which stretches from Caldey Island near Tenby to Worms Head on the Gower Peninsula. At low tide, extensive areas of sand are uncovered. Silting in the bay became an increasing problem during the nineteenth century and contributed to a decline in the prosperity of local ports.

Looking back across Scott's Bay to Wharley Point

Sands of time: *The spectacular ruins of Llansteffan Castle overlook the broad Towy Estuary*

6 From **Wharley Point**, a lovely path descends across steep wooded slopes to sea level at **Scott's Bay** and **St Anthony's Cottage**.

A short distance up a path to the left is 👁 **St Anthony's Well**. *Sixth-century Christian converts were baptised here by a Welsh hermit called Antwn — the Welsh form of Anthony. The holy well's waters were later reputed to have healing powers and attracted pilgrims travelling the King's Way to St David's.*

If the tide is out, it is possible to follow the beach around the headland to Llansteffan, but the official route continues across further wooded slopes below **Llansteffan Castle**. Descend to a public shelter and bear left along a gravel track. Llansteffan's main beach is now below on the right and can be accessed via a path forking right from the track. The official route continues along the track to a road.

Detour: *To visit Llansteffan Castle*
If you have the time, it is worth climbing the private drive on the left to **Llansteffan Castle**. *Entry is free and rewarded with splendid panoramic views from the castle mound.*

7 To continue on the **official route** for the Wales Coast Path, keep ahead up the road as far as a signpost and bench. From here, either carry on up the road into the centre of **Llansteffan village**, where there are pubs and a bus service to Carmarthen, or turn right, in the direction of the Wales Coast Path sign, and descend on a tarmac path to a car park and toilets on the **seafront**.

Salmon and sea trout

The River Towy or Tywi is the longest river flowing entirely through Wales. It's famous for its salmon, too, with good runs occurring each autumn. But it's best known for its sea trout or 'sewin', the seagoing form of the freshwater brown trout. Like salmon, sewin return to the Towy and its tributaries to breed, but in spring and early summer rather than autumn. With richer food available at sea, sewin are larger on average than riverine trout and much sought after by fishermen.

Llansteffan to Carmarthen

Distance: *9 miles / 15 kilometres* | **Start:** *Llansteffan SN 352 104* |
Finish: *Carmarthen SN 411 198* | **Maps:** *Ordnance Survey Explorer 177,*
Landranger 159

Outline: Another mainly inland section, crossing rolling hills towards the town of Carmarthen.

A mixture of tracks, field paths and minor roads takes the Wales Coast Path inland to the lowest crossing point of the Towy at Carmarthen. The route crosses undulating terrain, including two long, steep climbs: the first on the way out of Llansteffan and the second along a steep lane near Llangain. Both are rewarded with fine views along the Towy Estuary. The highlight of the section is a pleasant trail through Green Castle Woods Nature Reserve, an area of ancient woodland and meadow north-east of Llangain.

Services: *Tide permitting (summer only), there's now a ferry across the estuary to Ferryside, avoiding inland walking via Carmarthen. Llansteffan has a couple of pubs, a fish and chip shop, and a general store. There is also a post office and toilets, and a range of accommodation, including a campsite. Hotel and hostel at Pant yr Athro. Carmarthen TIC: 01267 231557 | carmarthentic@carmarthenshire.gov.uk. Guv's Taxis: 07811 111679*

Don't miss: Llansteffan Castle – splendid headland castle with fantastic panormamic views | **St Cain's Church, Llangain** – peaceful spot dedicated to a daughter of King Brychan of Brycheiniog | **Green Castle Woods Nature Reserve** – an area of ancient woodlands and meadow to the south of Carmarthen

▲ *Llansteffan Castle dominates the coast*

Llansteffan

The Normans captured the area around **Llansteffan** early in the twelfth century, constructing a defensive earth and timber structure on the site of a former Iron Age promontory fort. Nevertheless, even after being refortified in stone, the castle was subject to constant attack and occupation by Welsh forces. Following Llywelyn the Last's siege in 1257, two D-shaped corner towers were added to the castle, along with a striking double-towered gatehouse. Despite these improvements, the castle was still captured and held by Owain Glyndŵr at the beginning of the fifteenth century.

The village below the castle is notable for its attractive Georgian architecture and tranquil estuary setting. Llansteffan became a popular holiday destination after 1852, when the railway arrived in neighbouring Ferryside; a ferry transported visitors across the Towy. The village has also provided a haven for a number of Welsh writers, including Glyn Jones, a writer originally from Merthyr who is buried in the parish church.

Between the castle and the village sits the sixteenth-century mansion of Plas Llanstephan. Between 1903 and 1909, the house was home to Sir John Williams, a royal physician and collector of antique books and manuscripts who played a key role in founding the National Library of Wales.

Llansteffan Castle looms above the coastal trees

The route: **Llansteffan to Carmarthen**

👁 **Llansteffan Castle** is well worth a visit.

1 From the car park at the southern end of **Llansteffan village**, join a tarmac path along the seafront. On approaching playing fields, turn left through a second car park (toilets now closed) and keep ahead onto a road up the hill. When you reach a T-junction, cross to **Old School Road** and turn immediately right onto a tarmac drive. Continue through a gate onto an enclosed track.

Climb steeply on an enclosed **sunken track** between high hedges. *There is little to see for most of the ascent, but after the track levels off there is the occasional glimpse of Ferryside across the estuary.* Fork left where the track splits, immediately reaching a junction with the access lane to **'Lan Farm'**. Bear right onto the lane and descend to a T-junction with a minor road.

2 Follow the road left, then fork right at a left-hand bend onto a narrower, dead-end lane. Where the tarmac surface ends, turn right through double gates and join a track. Keep ahead along the right-hand edge of a field, then join a deeply rutted track. Where the track begins to descend along the left-hand boundary of a field, bear right and follow the right-hand field edge down to a gate and stile in the bottom corner.

Sand castle: *Llansteffan Castle draws the eye from far up the estuary*

Ignore the track ahead and turn sharp left onto a track enclosed along the bottom of the field. The trail then continues down the left-hand edge of fields and onto a grassy woodland path. Swing left along a rough track to a junction with a road and turn right.

3 Shortly reach a junction with the **B4312**. Turn left, then almost immediately left again onto a parallel path. Where directed, rejoin the main road and continue carefully until the start of a narrow lane on the right. Climb steeply, the gradient gradually levelling off as you ascend. Where electricity wires cross the road ahead, take the second of two closely spaced turnings on the right (the lane signed to the church). At the next junction, bear right and follow a lane past 👁 **St Cain's Church**.

In ecclesiastical terms, St Cain's is a relatively recent building, dating only from 1871. It replaced an older, medieval church that stood slightly to the south. This was also dedicated to St Cain, a female saint who was one of the twenty-four daughters of Brychan Brycheiniog, a fifth-century Welsh king. The parish of Llangain takes its name from the saint and the church she founded.

4 Just past the church, turn left onto a dead-end lane signed to 'Church Farm'. Follow a track downhill to **farm buildings** and ahead into a field. Bear slightly right; about halfway across, a kissing gate into the woods ahead

Dusk falls on Dylan Thomas' Boathouse

Dylan Thomas country

Dylan Thomas and the Carmarthen Bay and Gower coast

The sea is a recurring motif in Dylan Thomas' poems and stories, reflecting a long-standing personal connection with the coastal landscapes of Wales, particularly those of Swansea, Carmarthenshire and Gower.

The sea was an inescapable presence in Thomas' early life. The view from his childhood home in the Uplands, Swansea, is dominated by the long arc of Swansea Bay. As Thomas grew up, the foreshore, with its attractions and girls, became a natural place to loiter, whether alone or with friends. He later captured the listless atmosphere of these days in two short stories, 'One Warm Saturday' and 'Just Like Little Dogs'.

The Mumbles was also a draw, particularly when Thomas became

Dylan Thomas' writing shed, Laugharne

old enough to frequent the village's many pubs; two favourite haunts were the Antelope and the Mermaid (the first is now closed, the second a restaurant). Just round the headland are two popular bays, Langland and Caswell, to which Thomas and his friends would make regular outings on summer weekends.

As a boy, he also used to camp with a group of friends near Rhossili, an experience recreated with humour and pathos in 'Extraordinary Little Cough'. Another story, 'Who Do You Wish Was With Us?', describes a later, adolescent trip to Rhossili, in which Thomas and a friend become trapped on Worms Head after being cut off by the incoming tide.

As a child, Thomas was also a frequent visitor to Carmarthenshire, where both his parents had strong family ties. His mother's family were particularly numerous on the triangle of land between the Tâf and Towy estuaries. Thomas stayed with relatives in Llansteffan as a boy, but was a more frequent visitor to his Aunt Annie's farm Fernhill, near Llangain. It was childhood memories of Carmarthenshire that inspired one of his best-known poems, 'Fern Hill'.

On the other side of the Tâf is

Dylan Thomas, sculpture by John Doubleday in Swansea's Maritime Quarter

> *"Time held me green and dying / Though I sang in my chains like the sea."*
>
> Fern Hill, *Dylan Thomas*

Laugharne, the town in which Thomas lived for the final four years of his life. Much of his later poetry is imbued with the atmosphere and landscape of the town, and its characters almost certainly helped to inspire Llareggub, the fictional town ('bugger-all' backwards) in which *Under Milk Wood* is set.

Thomas is buried with his wife Caitlin in the new cemetery of Laugharne's parish church, in a grave marked by a simple white cross. The Boathouse, home for his last four years, is now a museum dedicated to his life and work.

More information: Stories mentioned can be found in Thomas' *Collected Stories*. For a readable account of Thomas' life, see Paul Ferris' *Dylan Thomas: The Biography* (revised ed., 1999).

Beauty in blue: *A haze of fragrant bluebells carpets the woodland floor in Greencastle Woods*

becomes visible. Aim for these and join a winding woodland track above the **River Towy**.

These woods alongside the Towy are part of the 👁 **Green Castle Woods Nature Reserve,** *an area of mainly oak woodland and meadows either side of the B4312. The reserve's name derives from Green Castle or Castell Moel, a prominent fortified mansion house overlooking the River Towy that is now an overgrown ruin.*

The reserve consists of a mix of ancient, semi-ancient and newly created woodlands, as well as a number of botanically rich meadows. The woods in May contain some of the best bluebell displays in the country, but the autumn colours of the deciduous oak and ash trees are just as spectacular. There is plenty of birdlife in the woods, though this is not always easy to see among the dense canopy. You may hear the harsh call of a jay or the tapping sound of a nuthatch wedging an acorn into the crevice of a tree.

Below the steep wooded slopes of **Allt Morfa-Howell** is a stretch of the **River Towy** known as the **Black Pool**.

Ships sailing upriver to Carmarthen would either wait at this point for the incoming tide to carry them up into the town or unload their cargoes onto smaller boats for the remaining journey.

Climb past a **carved bench** to a fork in the path. Take the lower, narrower path to the right, which continues through trees along a steep wooded bluff above the River Towy. Draw parallel to the main road, running above you to the left. Eventually, climb wooden steps to the road and cross carefully to a metal kissing gate on the far side.

Two weeks in summer

Back in the early 1900s, a regular ferry service operated between Llansteffan and the railway station in Ferryside. For a fortnight each summer, the boats were packed with holidaymakers, including miners and railway workers from across South Wales. Because the pits were shut for maintenance work, the holiday became known as 'Miners' Fortnight'. Entertainments laid on for Llansteffan's August Fair included eisteddfodau and a mock mayor-making ceremony.

5 Pass through further woodland below an **old quarry face**. Climb more steps and continue parallel to the road, now below on the right. As the path starts to climb left, away from the road, leave the woods by turning right towards a gate marked 'Parc Gwyn Bach'. Descend steps to the right of the gate and continue along a clear path through meadows.

During May and June, these wet meadows adjacent to Green Castle Woods are carpeted with wild flowers and awash with colour. Golds and yellows dominate (fleabane, bird's foot trefoil and meadow buttercup), but there are also splashes of purple (knapweed), pink (ragged robin) and various shades of cream (wild angelica and sneezewort).

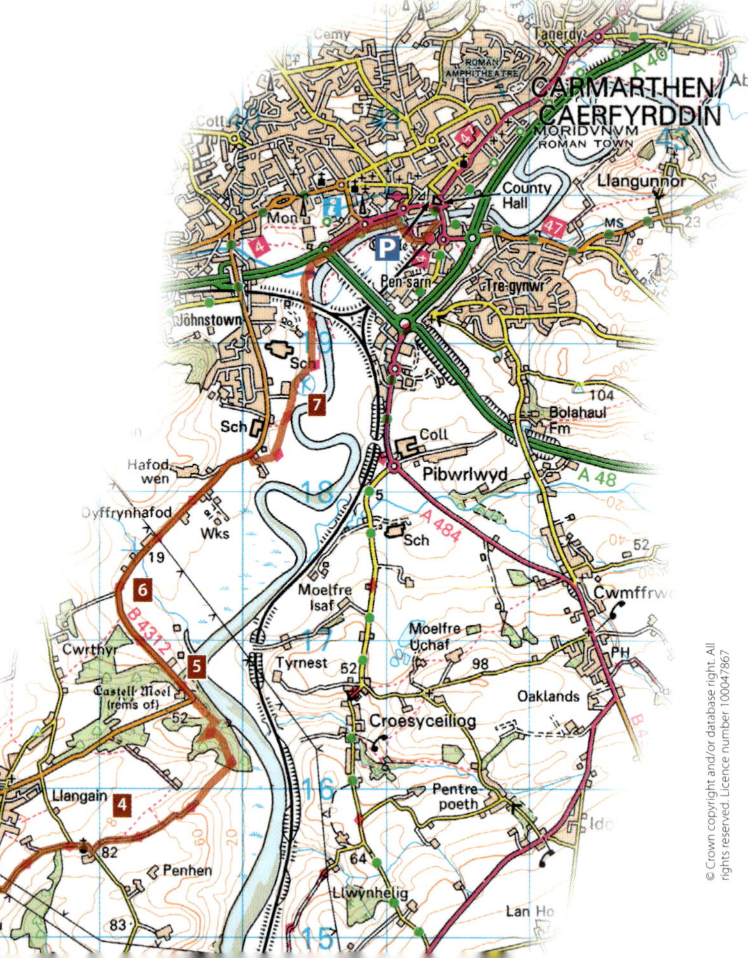

Winding river: *The River Towy meanders dramatically close to the centre of Carmarthen*

At the bottom of a long meadow, fork right and cross a stile back on to the main road.

6 Follow the grass verge alongside the main road for about 1 kilometre, until level with the farm road to **'Hafod-wen'**. Turn right opposite a telegraph pole on a triangle of grass and join an enclosed path parallel to the road. Turn right down an access road to **'Trysordy'** — a community and recycling centre — then left in the car park, passing through a kissing gate into **playing fields.** Follow the edge of the fields round to the far end and join a path by a wooden fence.

7 Cross a track to a footbridge and kissing gate. Any of the paths ahead will take you in the right direction, but the official route goes left to join a tarmac path behind school playing fields. With a car park to the left, bear right, following the path down towards the **River Towy**, then along its banks. Pass below the railway and busy A40 dual carriageway and continue to where the distinctive **Pont King Morgan footbridge** crosses the river. The section ends here, with **Carmarthen town centre** and bus station across the road to the left and the railway station and continuation of the Wales Coast Path across the bridge on the right.

Carmarthen to Kidwelly

Distance: *14 miles/ 22 kilometres* | **Start:** *Carmarthen SN 411 198*
Finish: *Kidwelly SN 407 067* | **Maps:** *Ordnance Survey Explorer 177, Landranger 159*

Outline: This section takes the Wales Coast Path across more rolling hills above the Towy and Gwendraeth estuaries.

The National Cycle Network provides a swift but unexciting route out of Carmarthen, initially alongside the A484, then via a minor road to Croesy-ceiliog. The Wales Coast Path then continues along a mixture of tracks, field paths and narrow country lanes to rejoin the River Towy at Ferryside. After crossing steep wooded slopes above the village, the path follows an undulating route to Llansaint, a hilltop village with fantastic views over Carmarthen Bay. An enclosed track drops steeply to a minor road and cycle path leading into Kidwelly.

Services: *Carmarthen is the largest town between Tenby and Swansea and contains plenty of accommodation, banks, post offices, shops, pubs and bars, restaurants, cafés and takeaways. There is a pub, shop, hotel, toilets and a post office in Ferryside, and a pub and campsite in Llansaint. Carmarthen TIC: 01267 231557 | carmarthentic@ carmarthenshire.gov.uk. Guv's Taxis: 07811 111679*

Don't miss: Carmarthen – oldest town in Wales, founded by the Romans | **Llansaint** – unusual hilltop village built round a maze of tiny streets | **Kidwelly Castle** – well-preserved castle above the Gwendraeth Fach river

▲ *The old bridge in the centre of Carmarthen*

Carmarthen

Carmarthen has a strong claim to be the oldest town in Wales, having been founded by the Romans in the first century AD. The town, *Moridunum*, seems to have been developed purposefully to create an administrative capital for the Demetae tribe, who under Roman law formed a civitas or self-governing republic. The only other example of such a civitas in Wales is the Silurian capital of Caerwent, west of Chepstow.

Following the collapse of Roman rule, the name *Moridunum* — which means fort by the sea — contracted to 'myrdin' or 'myrddin', based on the belief that the town was the birthplace of the legendary wizard Myrddin or Merlin. In reality, little seems to have happened in Carmarthen until the arrival of the Normans, who built a castle high above the River Towy at the beginning of the twelfth century. A town, called New Carmarthen, developed around the castle, combining as it expanded with the older settlement near St Peter's Church and the Augustinian priory founded in 1148.

By the sixteenth century, Carmarthen was an important port with more than 2,000 inhabitants and the largest town in Wales. Although no longer *'the chiefe citie of the country'*, as William Camden described it in 1586, Carmarthen today remains an unofficial capital for south-west Wales.

Approaching Carmarthen along the west bank of the River Towy

The route: Carmarthen to Kidwelly

1 After crossing the bridge from the centre of 👁 **Carmarthen**, follow the station access road as it curves left. Take a signed cycle path on the right, which turns sharply around the end of a siding and emerges on a minor road. Keep ahead alongside a main road, passing numerous garages.

At a mini-roundabout, turn left and pass below the busy A40. Immediately turn right onto **Emlyn Terrace**, continuing onto a tarmac **cycle path** at the end of the street. Go through a subway and climb to a main road (the A484) near a roundabout. Follow the pavement left, crossing to the opposite side of the road at traffic lights. Keep straight ahead at a roundabout, still following **Route 4 of the National Cycle Network**.

2 At the next roundabout in **Pibwrlwyd**, turn right, following the cycle signs for 'Kidwelly' and 'Llanelli'. The pavement comes to an end after **Ysgol Bro Myrddin** (Secondary school). Watching out for fast-moving traffic, continue into the countryside along a minor road.

3 After about 1.5 kilometres, you enter the small village of **Croesyceiliog**. Go through the village, turning right onto a dead-end lane about 500 metres after the last houses. Descend steeply in the direction of the estuary and pass a house. The lane becomes a track, which is initially

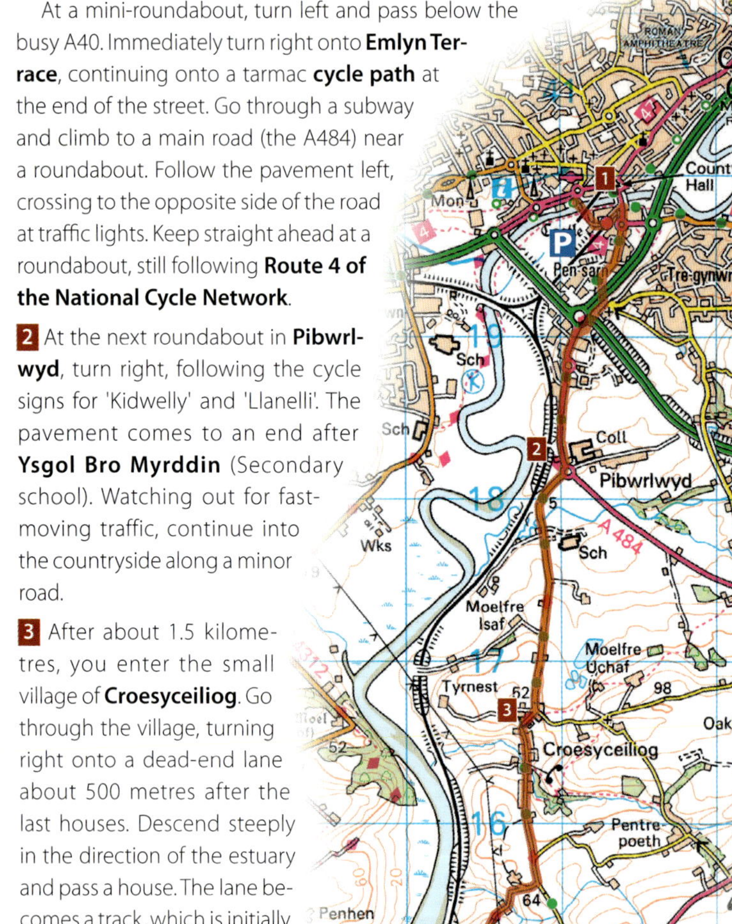

Seaside special: *The West Wales line runs alongside the pretty Towy estuary*

enclosed and then follows the left-hand edge of a field. After passing below electricity wires, the track curves left, crossing a stream and climbing to the right towards farm buildings.

4 Just before the farm, bear left into a field to bypass the buildings. Cross a **footbridge** and curve left into a field over a stile. Follow the right-hand edge of the field uphill until it is possible to go through a kissing gate on the right. Follow the fence along to another kissing gate, this time on the left. Head up the right-hand side of a field to a group of houses.

Bear left between the houses and then right along the access road away from them. This turns sharply left by **Towy Castle Residential Home** and meets a lane at a corner. Turn right and begin to descend. At a left-hand bend, keep straight ahead into the grounds of **Gellylednais**. Bear left across the garden to a self-closing gate in a hedge to emerge in a field.

5 Follow the right-hand edge of the field down to a lane. Cross over and drop down another field, curving right to a kissing gate on the left. A steep flight of steps descends into a narrow **wooded gulley** and a bridge across a stream. Climb out of the gulley and cross a field to pick up the line of a hedge towards **Pentrecwm Farm**. *There are good views from here back along the River Towy towards Carmarthen.*

6 Go through a kissing gate and join the access lane leading away from the farm. Stay on this road until a left-hand bend by **Trelimsy Farm** (marked 'Trelymsi' on the OS Explorer map). At this point, continue onto the lane directly ahead, which soon begins to descend towards the track of the **West Wales railway line**. Do not cross the line, but turn left onto a track towards a house named **Bronyn**. Bear right and then left between buildings and continue onto a lane on the far side.

7 As you crest a small brow, **Ferryside** becomes visible ahead. *Facing the village across the estuary is Llansteffan, the starting point for the previous Day Section.* The lane follows the railway closely to a junction with a wider road on the edge of the village. Turn right and walk through the long, linear village until you reach the railway station. *Close by are a general store, a pub and a licensed restaurant. There is a free car park and toilets, and it is possible to access a sandy beach across a level crossing.*

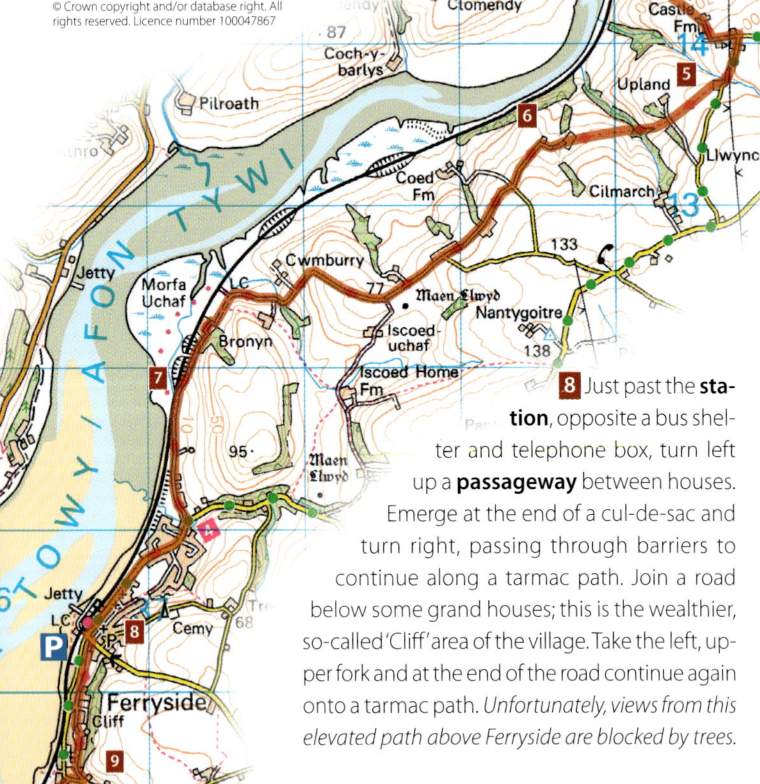

8 Just past the **station**, opposite a bus shelter and telephone box, turn left up a **passageway** between houses. Emerge at the end of a cul-de-sac and turn right, passing through barriers to continue along a tarmac path. Join a road below some grand houses; this is the wealthier, so-called 'Cliff' area of the village. Take the left, upper fork and at the end of the road continue again onto a tarmac path. *Unfortunately, views from this elevated path above Ferryside are blocked by trees.*

Looking across the River Towy from Ferryside to Llansteffan

Ferryside

A modern village on an ancient river crossing

As the name suggests, there has been a ferry at Ferryside for centuries. Indeed, the crossing formed part of an ancient route across South Wales known in medieval times as the King's Way. This route predates any settlement in Ferryside and followed the line of what is now a minor road climbing steeply over the hills to Kidwelly.

It was the arrival of the railway in 1852 that really put Ferryside on the map, transforming it from a small group of houses around the ferry crossing point into a sizeable village. At first, the railway line was laid across the shingle of the beach, but was soon rebuilt along a raised embankment to protect it from storms (one unfortunate effect of the embankment is to separate Ferryside from its beach).

A station allowed connections to be made with the Llansteffan ferry and also provided employment for porters, signalmen, ticket clerks and others. By 1856, Ferryside was large enough to support a school and was also beginning to attract wealthier residents. These tended to settle along the attractive wooded slopes of 'The Cliff', an area of steeply rising ground to the south of the station, high above the level of the railway embankment.

More information: A walking guide to the Ferryside area is published by Carmarthenshire County Council | www.carmarthenshire.gov.uk

Along the marsh: *A West Wales train approaches Kidwelly alongside the marshy Gwendraeth*

The path turns to gravel, then joins a track running down to a road. Turn right downhill then shortly left onto a road signed to 'Llansaint' and 'Kidwelly'. After about 150 metres, pass a driveway and turn left up a short flight of **stone steps** followed by a distinctive **metal staircase.**

Alternative route: *Low level road route to Kidwelly*

If you would prefer to avoid the steep climbs and descents of the inland route via Llansaint, it is possible to follow the lane along the coast to Kidwelly. However, be aware that this can be a busy road, particularly in summer.

9 Climb through trees to a field and keep ahead to a kissing gate. Continue along the right-hand edge of fields until you reach a gate leading to an enclosed path below trees. Cross a **footbridge** over a stream and shortly join a track by a house. Bear left to a kissing gate into a field.

Follow the right-hand field edge to its end, then bear left to a gateway. Go through and keep ahead for a short distance. Bear left to a second gateway and continue uphill along the left-hand edge of a field. Join a track towards **Pengay Farm**, keeping ahead onto a lane in front of the farm buildings.

This grand farmhouse was home during the eighteenth century to a prominent Methodist family called the Bevans. Entrance to the farmyard is through an arched gateway containing a bell dated 1760, salvaged from a wrecked Dutch ship.

10 A little over 200 metres along the lane, turn right through a kissing gate and descend along the right-hand edge of a field. Drop steeply on a stepped path into a **wooded valley**, turning left along a lane at the bottom. Almost

Medieval hilltop village

The unusual hilltop village of Llansaint consists of terraces built around a maze of tiny streets. The focus of the village is its twelfth-century church, which was built on a possible Iron Age site. Memorial stones built into the walls suggest that the first Christian settlement predates the present building by a number of centuries. The stones commemorate two Dark Age chieftains or priests of possible Irish origin, Vennisettl and Cimesetl, and date from the fifth or sixth century.

Timeless town: *Kidwelly is a pleasant Welsh town with traditional shops and pubs*

immediately, go through a foot gate on the right and follow a path climbing steeply out of the valley. After a kissing gate, climb more gently along the right-hand edge of a field. Keep ahead between houses to a track, then bear left along a lane into the hilltop village of 👁 **Llansaint**.

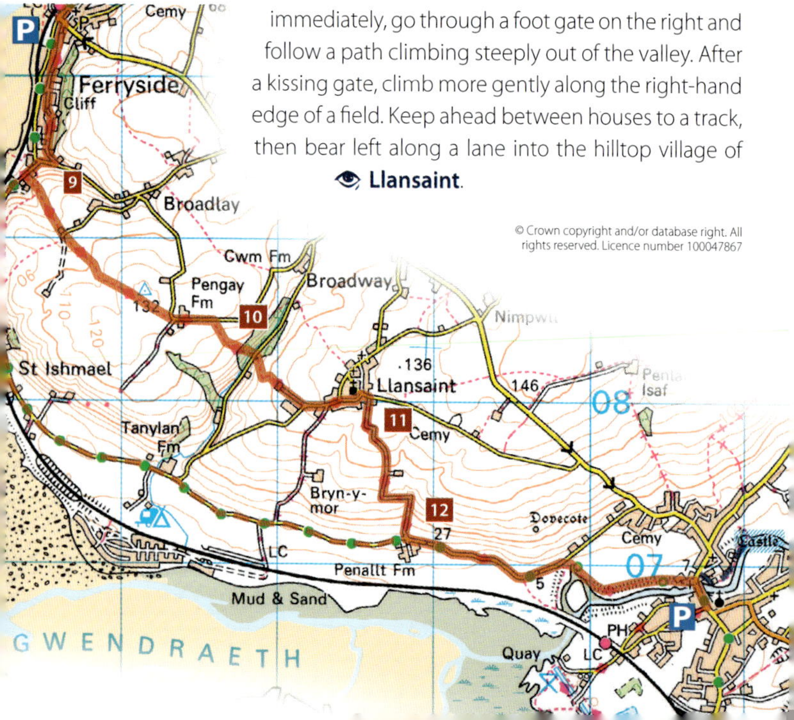

   The Wales Coast Path follows a road along the bottom edge of the village (the church and **Kings Arms** pub are up a narrow road on the left). At a junction with a wider road opposite **Ty Mawr**, bear right, away from the village. Just past the last houses, turn right onto a narrow tarmac lane by **public toilets**.

11 The lane begins to descend, at first gradually, then more steeply, towards the sea. Continue ahead at **Parc-cwm** onto a grassy track. Swing left, then right, and descend steeply again to meet the lane from Ferryside opposite **Penallt farmhouse**.

12 Follow this sometimes busy lane to the left for a little over 1 kilometre. Where it starts to climb and curve left, turn right onto a **tarmac cycle path**. This meets the main road through **Kidwelly** by a bridge over the **Gwendraeth Fach**. Turn right and cross the bridge into Kidwelly (or keep ahead on a riverside path to visit 👁 **Kidwelly Castle**). The Coast Path continues down the next turning on the right, **Station Road**, passing the railway station on the edge of town (see next section for details).

The Gwendraeth Fach below Kidwelly Castle

Kidwelly to Burry Port

Distance: *10 miles / 17 kilometres* | **Start:** *Kidwelly SN 407 067* | **Finish:** *Burry Port SN 444 004* | **Maps:** *Ordnance Survey Explorer 177 & 164, Landranger 159*

Outline: A short, level section along a historic canal, splendid sandy beach and through two country parks.

The section begins with a pleasant detour around Kidwelly Quay and along the towpath of the Kymer Canal. The Wales Coast Path then rejoins the National Cycle Network, initially alongside the A484 and then along a concrete track across flat, marshy grazing. The path continues through Pembrey Forest and out on to Cefn Sidan Sands, a splendid beach which is followed south to Pembrey Country Park. After meandering through the country park, you will enter the Millennium Coastal Park, enjoying excellent views of the Loughor Estuary until the end of the section in Burry Port.

Services: *There are pubs, cafés, takeaways, a post office, cash point and a general store in Kidwelly, as well as B&Bs and hotels. There are campsites near Kidwelly and in Pembrey Country Park. The country park also contains a visitor centre, café and toilets. Llanelli TIC (Discovery Centre): 01554 777744 | discoverycentre@carmarthenshire.gov. uk. Kidwelly Cabs: 07766 836761*

Don't miss: **The Kymer Canal** – eighteenth-century canal built by local industrialist Thomas Kymer | **Cefn Sidan** – eight-mile long sandy beach between the Gwendraeth and Loughor rivers | **Pembrey Millennium Country Park** – popular country park set against the spectacular backdrop of the Gower Peninsula

▲ *Looking across the estuary from Cefn Sidan dunes*

Kidwelly

As elsewhere on the Carmarthenshire coast, the Normans invaded the area surrounding Kidwelly early in the twelfth century, building a castle of mud and timber close to where the town later developed. The castle was attacked and occupied by the Welsh on a number of occasions, though the most famous assault, by an army led by the princess consort of Deheubarth, Gwenllian ferch Gruffydd, failed to dislodge the Normans and resulted in the capture and beheading of Gwenllian herself. In the thirteenth century, the castle came into the possession of the de Chaworth family, who set about rebuilding the stronghold into the imposing stone structure visible today.

During the medieval period, the town became a centre for the woollen industry, which had been started by Flemish settlers in the twelfth century. Along the South Wales coast, Kidwelly's port was rivalled only by that of Carmarthen, until silting began to impede navigation along the Gwendraeth in the sixteenth century. Coal and tinplate revived the port's fortunes in the eighteenth century, with a canal being constructed to improve navigation. Tinplate continued to be produced in the town until the 1940s, though by then the quay had fallen into almost complete disuse.

Kidwelly Castle sits on a grassy ridge overlooking the Gwendraeth Estuary

Sand and forest: *Cefn Sidan Sands fringe Pembrey Forest and Pembrey Burrows*

The route: Kidwelly to Burry Port

1 Heading south into **Kidwelly** over the **Gwendraeth Fach**, take the next street on the right, **Station Road**. Pass a post office and then turn right into **Hillfield Villas** (also signed to the 'Gwenllian Centre'). Follow the road to a pub (Anthony's Hotel) opposite the **railway station** at the edge of town. Continue over the level crossing onto a country lane (trains to Ferryside and Carmarthen depart from this side of the line) and follow signs for 'car park' to the right.

2 Go through the car park and round the end of the 👁 **Kymer Canal** at **Kidwelly Quay**. Turn back on yourself, so that the picnic site is to your right, and follow the gravel **towpath** alongside the canal.

At a **stone bridge**, cross to the opposite bank so as to continue along the better quality gravel path. Go through a metal gate at the end of the canal and continue along a field edge with a railway to your left. Bear left up concrete steps and join a grassy track over the **railway line**. Pass the 'bed and breakfast' signs at **Caernewydd Farm** to reach a junction with a busy road. Follow the pavement to the right, in the direction of a roundabout.

3 As the road curves left to the roundabout, keep ahead onto the signed **cycleway**, which continues alongside the A484. About 600 metres along, swing right, passing below the railway. The cycle path continues along a raised **embankment**, with marshy grazing to the right.

4 Where signed, leave the embankment by turning left down a flight of steps towards a concrete track. Turn right and follow the track that runs

Coal, canals and quays

Built by local industrialist Thomas Kymer in the 1760s, the Kymer Canal was one of the first commercial canals in South Wales. Stretching for some 5 kilometres / 3 miles, the canal connected Kidwelly Quay with coal pits higher up the Gwendraeth Fawr valley at Pwll-y-llygod and Carway. In 1832, the canal was extended eastwards to newly built docks at Burry Port, effectively sealing the demise of Kidwelly as a major port.

parallel to the embankment. Before
long, this swings left, away from the
embankment, and curves sharply right
and then left to reach a track junction near
a motor racing circuit (the circuit is concealed
by trees but can be clearly heard when in use).
Turn right towards **Pembrey Forest**, a large pine
plantation established in the 1930s to stabilise the dune
system behind 👁 **Cefn Sidan Sands**.

At the first fork in the forest, keep ahead along the narrower concrete track, which soon starts to curve left. Ignore a track to the left, instead keeping ahead towards the sea. At the end of the concrete road, either bear left along the top of the sand dunes (if the tide is in) or walk through the dunes and out onto the beach.

5 Follow the **beach** left for about 4 kilometres. At this point, look out for a **track leaving the beach** just past some benches. Follow this up to a **lifeguard station**, **toilets** and **café,** and join a tarmac road. Bear right past some old anchors and then left, passing 👁 **Pembrey Country Park Visitor Centre**. Join a waymarked path, crossing a road and passing the entrance to the **miniature railway**. Cross another road and follow the waymarked stone pathway across a green and through a forest. Emerge in a field and head towards the **ski slope**. Immediately past the ski slope, at its eastern end, head up the hill on the left to the viewpoint car park.

6 Continue across the car park and descend across an open grassy area. Maintain direction, passing a **council depot** on your left, and rejoin a tarmac road. Bear left for 100 metres to reach a sharp left-hand bend. Turn right here, passing a Wales Coast Path interpretation panel, and continue between stones onto a gravel cycle path through the **Millennium Coastal Park**.

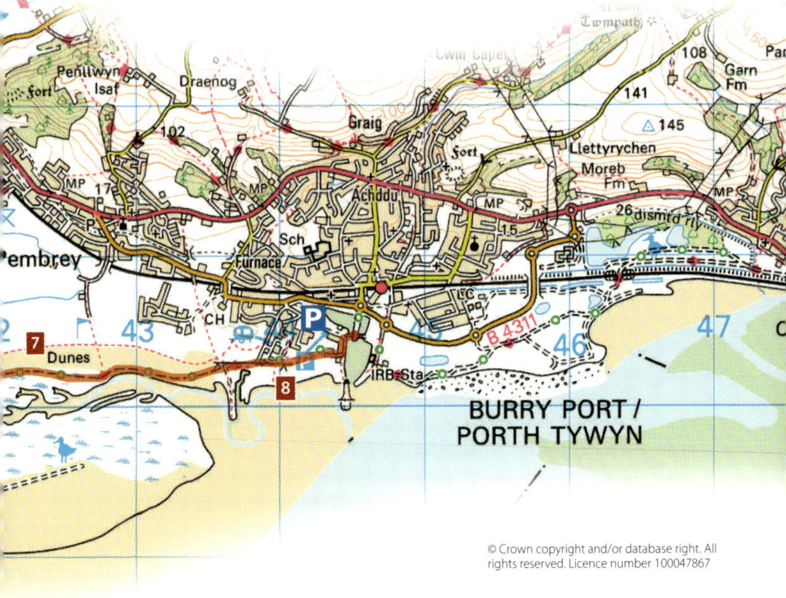

Cefn Sidan Sands with Burry Holms and Worms Head on the horizon

Sand, silt and shipwrecks

Cefn Sidan Sands and the silting up of Carmarthen Bay

To the unknowing eye, the vast expanses of sand revealed in Carmarthen Bay at low tide look like a permanent feature of the area's seascape. They are, however, a relatively recent phenomenon, and would have been far less prominent even two or three centuries ago. Some 6,000 years before this, the sea would have lapped the foot of the high ground behind Pembrey and Laugharne, and the large sand bars described by later mariners such as Captain Armstrong would have been considerably smaller, if there at all. By the Middle Ages, natural processes of deposition were being accelerated by building sea walls and draining the land with dykes, but it was still not until around 1800 that the coast began to settle into its current outline.

Increased rates of deposition and siltation affected not only the shape

19th-century wreck on Cefn Sidan Sands

of the coast, but also the depth and navigability of Carmarthen Bay and its estuaries. As Armstrong noted in 1878, the bay's tidal sand bars were the cause of numerous shipwrecks. Prevailing westerly winds would drive vessels into the bay's shallow waters during stormy weather, where they would founder and sink, leading Cefn Sidan Sands to be dubbed 'the dustbin of the Atlantic'. Local people were not averse to profiting from these occurrences, plundering wrecked ships and even deliberately luring them ashore through the lighting of fires. Men from Pembrey came to be known as Gwŷr y Bwyelli Bach ('People of the Little Axes') because of the tomahawk-style hatchets which they used to plunder shipwrecks and, according to some accounts, finish off any sailors still alive.

It was on the prosperity of Carmarthen Bay's ports that the long-term impacts of siltation were felt. In medieval times, Kidwelly was a major port, rivalling Carmarthen as South Wales's busiest harbour; even as late as 1797, Kidwelly Quay could accept vessels drawing up to 5.5 metres (18 feet) of water with ease. At the other end of Cefn Sidan Sands, Pembrey, too,

Cefn Sidan Sands with the Gower behind

> *"The treacherous Cefn Sidan Sands extended miles out to sea; and at low water appeared like an immense desert of sand ..."*

Captain Armstrong's description of Cefn Sidan Sands, 1878

briefly flourished as an industrial port in the early nineteenth century, though today its former harbour is no more than a muddy inlet. Continual silting along the Gwendraeth and Loughor estuaries led to a decline in these two ports, with maritime activity moving to new, purpose-built harbours at Burry Port and Llanelli. Shipping channels here were kept open by dredging, an activity that may itself have led to increased siltation rates in older, neighbouring harbours.

More information: An information booklet, 'Historical Relics of Cefn Sidan', has been produced by Carmarthenshire County Council and is on sale at Pembrey Country Park (01554 742424).

Sand and sea: *A gull's-eye view over the tidal sands of the Loughor Estuary to distant Pembrey*

Alternative route: *Continuing along the beach*

If you prefer to bypass the country park, it is possible to continue along the beach for a further kilometre or so. Take the next wide sandy track on the left and follow this through dunes to a road. Keep ahead as far as a sharp left-hand bend, then bear right to join the gravel cycle path through the Millennium Coastal Park.

7 As you continue through the coastal park, the views open out, and you will be able to see the Gower Peninsula clearly across the tidal inlet on your right. Keep ahead at a cross-path where a jetty stretches out towards the sea.

The end of the jetty lies directly opposite **Whiteford Point** *on the Gower Peninsula and marks the entrance to the* **Loughor Estuary**. *The muddy inlet to the east is all that remains of Pembrey Harbour. In the early nineteenth century, Pembrey briefly flourished as an industrial port before being displaced in 1832 by a new, purpose-built harbour at Burry Port, a short distance along the coast.*

8 Bear slightly right through a parking area to continue to the seaward side of a **caravan park**. Shortly after forking left on the far side of the caravans, leave the cycle route by turning right across rough ground to a lane by a derelict house. Emerge alongside the newly established **Burry Port Marina** and follow the water's edge to the left. There are toilets at the far end of the marina, as well as ample car parking.

To access **Burry Port** — with its railway station, bus stops and wide range of facilities — cross the footbridge on the right and turn immediately left.

Millennium Coastal Park

The Millennium Coastal Park occupies some 20km/12 miles of former industrial wasteland along the mouth of the River Loughor, between Pembrey and Bynea. The park offers a continuous traffic-free walkway and cycleway (the Millennium Coastal Path), now incorporated into the Wales Coast Path. The pathway runs along a coastal strip of green parkland with excellent views across the Loughor to the Gower Peninsula.

Burry Port to Loughor

Distance: *11 miles / 17 kilometres* | **Start:** *Burry Port SN 444 004* | **Finish:** *Loughor SS 563 980* | **Maps:** *Ordnance Survey Explorer 164, Landranger 159*

Outline: A level section along the Loughor Estuary, mostly following a shared cycleway through the Millennium Coastal Park.

Most of this section follows a cycle path within the boundaries of the Millennium Coastal Park, though there are stretches of unpaved parallel paths for walkers. The park comprises an area of reclaimed industrial wasteland along the Loughor Estuary and offers excellent views of the north Gower coast. At Bynea, you leave the park and continue along a residential road to Loughor Bridge. The A484 takes the Wales Coast Path across the river estuary to the section end in Loughor.

Services: *There's a wide range of services in both Burry Port and Llanelli, including pubs, takeaways, general stores, banks, post offices, toilets, cash points, pharmacies, B&Bs and hotels. Llanelli TIC (Discovery Centre): 01554 777744 | discoverycentre@ carmarthenshire.gov.uk. Andy's Taxis: 01554 741373*

Don't miss: **Burry Port Marina** – attractive modern marina in a former industrial port | **Discovery Centre, Llanelli** – find out more about the Millennium Coastal Park, the UK's largest land reclamation project | **Llanelli Wetland Centre** – extensive nature reserve run by the Wildfowl and Wetlands Trust

▲ *Burry Port harbour*

Burry Port

As a town, **Burry Port** is a fairly recent development, dating only from the middle of the nineteenth century. Prior to that, it was the adjacent village of Pembrey, around the old parish church, that was the main population centre.

Pembrey itself expanded rapidly during the eighteenth and early nineteenth centuries, when it acted as a port for coal mined in the nearby Gwendraeth valley. However, its harbour was prone to silting and in 1832 a new harbour — at first named Pembrey New Harbour but later renamed Burry Port Harbour — was built a short distance along the coast.

By 1850, a town was developing rapidly around these new docks, which were capable of handling ships of up to 1,860 tonnes. When the railway arrived two years later, it was at Burry Port, rather than Pembrey, that the local station was sited. As well as exporting coal, the new town of Burry Port developed its own copper and tinplate works and, from the 1880s, began to manufacture explosives.

By the end of the twentieth century, almost all the industries that had made Burry Port a town had closed. Its original purpose gone, Burry Port Harbour has recently been converted into an attractive modern marina.

Burry Port's iconic stubby lighthouse

The route: **Burry Port to Loughor**

1 From the car park on the west side of 👁 **Burry Port Marina**, cross the two footbridges at the top end and turn right towards the sea. Follow the edge of the marina past a car park on the left and join a **wide tarmac path** above a sandy beach. At the far end of a long parking area, bear left, slightly away from the sea, onto another wide tarmac path.

The Wales Coast Path continues along **Route 4 of the National Cycle Network**, passing through an area of reclaimed industrial wasteland containing a number of small lakes. Just after reaching a **picnic area** close to the estuary, fork left in order to cross to the landward side of the railway line.

The bridge over the railway consists of grassy terraces designed to blend in with the natural landscape. A phenomenal amount of landscaping has been completed throughout the coastal park, an area that had been blighted by heavy industry since the nineteenth century. The project to reclaim this former industrial wasteland for leisure use was the largest of its kind ever undertaken in the UK.

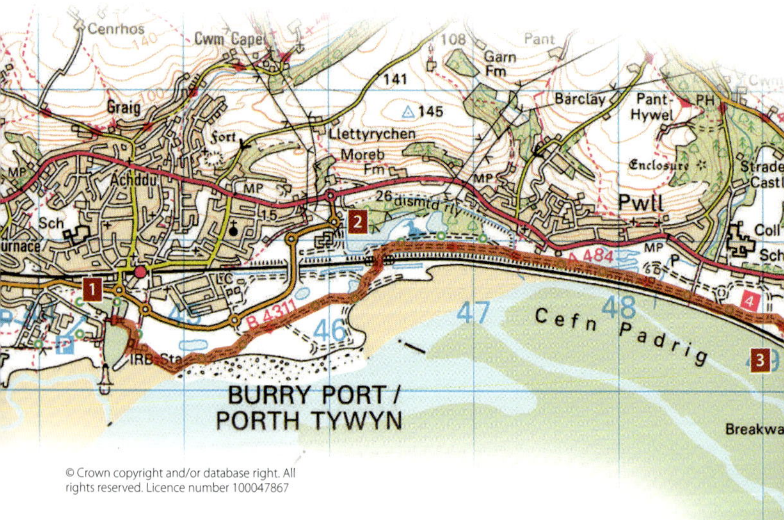

2 Straight after the bridge, leave the main cycle route by turning right onto a grassy path alongside the railway. Keep ahead onto a gravel track running parallel to the line with the estuary waters a short distance beyond. The tarmac cycle path is rejoined a short distance before a former cricket pitch in **Pwll**.

Pastel hues?: *A mother and daughter enjoy pedalling along the coastal cycleway*

The cricket pavilion is now a café. A plaque nearby commemorates the spot where in June 1928 Amelia Earhart landed her plane in the estuary near Pwll. She had flown solo across the Atlantic Ocean, the first woman to do so.

Keep ahead across a mini-roundabout built around a **sculpted red dragon**, then swing right onto a red tarmac path climbing back over the railway (the left fork alongside the lake will take you into the centre of Llanelli). Do not be misled by a waymark indicating that Swansea is only 13 miles away; the cycleway follows a much more direct route than the Coast Path!

3 Drop to the front and continue above a muddy beach. Ignore signs directing cyclists left and keep ahead along the shore to the 👁 **Discovery Centre**, which hosts a **tourist information centre** and **café**. Bear left past the building, then turn left across an access road to a car park. Follow the pavement left and continue alongside a road. Cross a bridge over the **dock entrance** and then a **footbridge** across a tidal pill. The pavement swings right, passing close to a roundabout.

Llanelli railway station can be reached by keeping straight ahead across the roundabout onto Marine Street.

4 The Coast Path continues along a wide cycleway between a busy road and a tidal inlet, the former **Copper Works Dock**. Continue past a roundabout and cross a wooden bridge. Just after the bridge, follow the cycle signs right towards the coast (the path may be diverted here due to building work) and continue on a path between the estuary and a new housing development.

5 Continue to follow the estuary until you are directed left, away from the coast and to the right of a fairly substantial **lake**. Beyond the lake is **Machynys Peninsula Golf Club**.

Just after crossing a ditch, some respite from the relentless tarmac can be found by joining an elevated parallel path to the right. Another advantage to this path is that it allows you to see over the sea wall and across the marshes to the coast. The bike path is rejoined at the end of the stone wall and continues inland towards **Trostre Steelworks**, a rare survival from Llanelli's industrial heyday.

6 Before reaching the works, the path swings right below electricity wires. Draw alongside a busy road and reach a junction with an old lane, now sliced in two by the new main road. Turn right along the lane, shortly crossing the access road to the 👁 **National Wetlands Centre**. Continue onto a path signed to 'Bynea Gateway'.

Machynys and the Loughor Estuary seen from the air

Monks, tinplate and golf

Former tinplate community on a monastic island

This area is known as Machynys, a name that may be derived from the Welsh words for 'monks' and 'island'. Old maps show that the land on which Machynys stands was indeed an island prior to the nineteenth century; tradition also states that a medieval monastery was founded by a St Piro here during the 'Age of Saints'. The seventeenth-century Machynys House, which later became known as Machynys Farm, was said to have been built on the site of the monastery. The farm was demolished in the 1970s, but was said to have a tunnel that extended beneath the River Loughor all the way to the north Gower coast.

Although originally a rural area, prone to flooding by the River Loughor, Machynys became heavily industrialised during the latter half of the nineteenth century. After sea defences were strengthened, tinplate works were established and a small village called Bwlch y Gwynt grew up nearby. The village was abandoned after the closure of the works in the 1960s and was later removed. After years of dereliction, the area has recently been transformed, with the development of a prestigious golf club and an exclusive waterside village.

More information:
Details of industrial Machynys can be found at:
www.abandonedcommunities.co.uk

Coastal corridor: *The Millennium Coastal Park cycleway is hugely popular with walkers and cyclists*

7 The path rejoins the estuary edge opposite the village of Pen-clawdd. As you round a right-hand bend, there is another opportunity to join a parallel path alongside the sea wall. This eventually rejoins the cycle path for good opposite the **Gateway Caravan Park**.

8 The **Loughor Bridge** is now clearly visible ahead. After passing above marshy ground along a raised boardwalk, the path climbs onto a footbridge, crossing the main **West Wales railway line** and, immediately after, the **A484**.

Once across the bridge, swing right and then turn left onto a concrete lane. Shortly, turn right and pass through the **Bynea Gateway** car park. This marks the eastern end of the **Millennium Coastal Park**.

9 Go through the car park entrance and cross carefully to continue along a residential road opposite. Pass the **Lewis Arms** and continue past a play area on the right. Turn right opposite a factory and follow a path between a car park and housing estate. Climb steps up to the **A484** and follow the pavement left across the **Loughor Bridge**.

At a mini-roundabout on the far side, bear left and immediately cross the road to the opposite pavement (for the riverside car park, stay on the left-hand pavement). Follow the pavement left as far as the first street on the right, **Station Road**.

Llanelli Wetland Centre

The Llanelli Wetland Centre is one of ten wetland nature reserves in the UK managed by the Wildfowl and Wetlands Trust. Their reserve near Llanelli consists of 450 acres of lakes, streams and lagoons along the shores of the Loughor estuary — a diverse range of habitats attracting a wealth of plants and animals. One of the reserve's successes are the breeding little egrets, a species of small white heron once extinct in Britain but now increasing in numbers.

Loughor to Llanmadoc

Distance: *13 miles / 21 kilometres* | **Start:** *Loughor SS 563 980* | **Finish:** *Llanmadoc SS 447 936* | **Maps:** *Ordnance Survey Explorer 164, Landranger 159*

Outline: A generally level section dominated by a vast open salt marsh along the Loughor Estuary.

The section begins in north Gower's former industrial area, passing through villages once associated with mining and other industries: Loughor, Gowerton, Pen-clawdd and Crofty. Beyond Crofty you enter a rural landscape, part of Gower's designated Area of Outstanding Natural Beauty (AONB). Surfaces vary, with tarmac predominating to Llanrhidian, field paths between here and Landimore, then rough marshland track to Llanmadoc. The scenery improves during the day, the stretch below North Hill Tor being particularly attractive.

Services: *There are plenty of places to buy food, with pubs in Loughor, Gowerton, Pen-clawdd, Crofty and Llanrhidian; fish and chip shops in Gowerton and Penclawdd; and shops in Loughor, Gowerton, Pen-clawdd and Llanrhidian. Accommodation wise, there are B&Bs in Loughor, Pen-clawdd and Llanrhidian. There are also post offices in Loughor, Gowerton, Pen-clawdd, Crofty and Llanrhidian; cash points in Gowerton, Pen-clawdd and Llanrhidian; and a pharmacy in Pen-clawdd. Swansea TIC: 01792 468321 | tourism@swansea.gov.uk. Swallow Travel: 01792 898888.*

Don't miss: Llanrhidian – pretty rural village with several historic buildings
Weobley Castle – a fortified manor house overlooking the Loughor Estuary
Bovehill Castle – hilltop ruin with great views across the salt marshes of north Gower

▲ *Weobley Castle is a rare fortified manor house overlooking the marshes*

Loughor

Around AD 70, the Romans established a fort — *Leucarum* — at the lowest crossing point on the River Loughor. Over a thousand years later, at the beginning of the twelfth century, a new set of conquerors, the Normans, built a ringwork defensive structure on top of the old fort, emphasising the strategic significance of the site. The Welsh, too, recognised its importance, attacking and burning the Norman stronghold on several occasions during the twelfth and early thirteenth centuries. Later in the medieval period, the castle declined in importance, though it was nevertheless strengthened by the addition of a stone tower around 1300.

Although overshadowed by Swansea, **Loughor** prospered as a port in later times and developed a flourishing tin and steel industry during the nineteenth century. In 1852, the railway was extended from Swansea to Carmarthen and a viaduct built at Loughor to carry the line across the estuary (the modern Lougher Rail Viaduct was originally a wooden structure designed by Brunel). However, it was 1923 before Loughor was connected to Carmarthenshire by a permanent road bridge. Both structures, road and rail, lie close to the old fording point across the river.

A beached lifeboat on the Loughor Estuary

Sunset, sea rise: *The incoming tide creeps across the Loughor Estuary*

The route: **Loughor to Llanmadoc**

1 From **Loughor Bridge**, follow the **A4120** into Loughor along the right-hand pavement and take the first street on the right, called **Station Road**. Where the road ends, continue onto a narrow tarmac cycle path close to the busy **A484**. This passes below the remains of **Loughor Castle** and across playing fields to a road. Bear slightly right to continue onto a road opposite.

At the end of the road, keep ahead onto a wide cycle path to the right of houses and below the A484. This reaches a junction with a busy minor road, which the cycle route (but not the coast path) follows to the right. Cross the road and go through a traffic barrier onto an enclosed track. Where the main track bears right into a field, keep ahead and follow a pleasant tree-lined bridle path to where a footpath crosses the route. Turn right along the footpath, over a footbridge and level crossing, then past a farm. Turn left on to a narrower road which can be quite busy at rush hour.

2 At a junction, follow the road round a right-hand bend and across **Afon Lliw**. The road is now wider but potentially busier. Cross the entrance to a caravan site and negotiate a narrow corner. The road then climbs between houses to a signalled junction with the **B4295**. Cross the junction to **Brynymor Road**, which curves left into **Gowerton**.

For **Gowerton railway station**, *continue along Brynymor Road into the centre of Gowerton. Keep straight ahead at crossroads, then shortly bear left at a mini-roundabout onto* **Sterry Road** *(signed locally to 'Waunarlwydd' and 'Fforestfach'). At a junction with the* **B4295**, *keep ahead past the* **Commercial Hotel** *into* **Station Road**. *The train station is a short distance ahead at the end of the street.*

To continue on the official Wales Coast Path, bear immediately right as you enter **Brynymor Road** to join a path alongside a culverted stream. Follow the stream to a waymarked fork. Turn right and keep ahead below trees. Stay with the lower, right-hand path, ignoring any unsigned paths climbing to the left (though the correct path does eventually curve left up the slope itself). On emerging in a field, head straight across and join a track through woods. At a junction with a minor road, turn right downhill.

3 Just before a pavement appears alongside the road, turn left up **Llwyn-mawr Lane**. Continue onto an enclosed track below trees until you emerge in front of a house. Bear left and continue between buildings to a gate into a field. Follow the left-hand field boundary to a gate, then continue up the side of the next field to a gate at the top. Do not go through this gate, but turn right along the top edge of the field to a stile at the far end.

Saltmarsh silence: *Pen-clawdd's open marshes provide superb habitat for waders and wildfowl*

Continue onto a narrow path along the top of a bank until a farm track is reached and followed downhill. The track becomes a lane and curves right to a junction with the **B4295** by a restaurant. Cross the road to a metal gate a few metres to the right and bear left onto the **cycle path** — part of the **North Gower Trail** — running below the main road.

4 Rejoin the main road by '**Gower Timber**' industrial units and follow the pavement past a mini-roundabout into **Pen-clawdd**. The road swings sharply right and then left, passing a parking area along the estuary front.

Walk through the car park and onto a pavement at the far end. The houses on the right soon end and views open out across the marshes again. After passing the **Royal Oak**, there is a second line of houses, then more open views where the pavement divides into two. Further houses appear on approaching Crofty.

5 Shortly, take the first of two closely-spaced roads on the right into an industrial estate. Straight after the '**Gower Vehicle Test Centre**', turn right onto an enclosed path between hedges, which runs out to a kissing gate leading onto the **open marsh**. Go through and follow the edge of the marsh left.

A path forking right gives you the option of walking out to the end of the structure marked 'Slipway' on Ordnance Survey Explorer map.

The Wales Coast Path, though, continues along the marsh edge, joining a track used by local cocklers. Take the left fork (the right-hand track continues out to the cockle beds on the estuary mud) and follow the edge of the village back inland to where a **footbridge** crosses the muddy **Salthouse Pill**

Pen-clawdd

Sparsely populated in medieval times, Pen-clawdd became an important port in the seventeenth century, exporting coal, cockles, copper and tinplate, on ships that were often built locally. But a shift in the River Loughor's main channel in the late 1800s made the village inaccessible to all but small boats, and the export of seafood and industrial products was taken over by the newly arrived railway.

/ **Morlais River** near a children's play area. Turn right onto a lane running along the edge of **Llanrhidian Marsh** (or left for the **Crofty Inn**).

Stretching almost the entire length of Gower's north coast, this extensive salt marsh provides an important winter habitat for ducks, geese and waders, as well as grazing for numerous wild ponies. The sheep raised on these salty pastures are also highly prized, with 'salt marsh lamb' being considered particularly tasty.

6 The lane, which can sometimes be flooded at high tide, follows the edge of the marsh for close to 5 kilometres. As you approach Llanrhidian, you will pass below the distinctive outline of **Cilifor Top**.

Detour: *To visit Iron Age hillfort on Cilifor Top*

This Iron Age hillfort, which covers an area of almost eight acres, is the largest on the Gower Peninsula and was one of the most strongly defended. The inner fort is surrounded by three concentric bank-and-ditch defensive structures and the extensive views along the north Gower coast would have given early warning of any enemy approach by sea.

Little is known about the relationship between the Romans and the Celtic tribes of the Gower Peninsula. The latter may have been defeated militarily or quickly accommodated themselves to Roman rule. Whichever was the case, the Romans must have found the towering ramparts of Cilifor Top an imposing sight as they sailed to and from their garrison post at nearby Leucarum (Loughor).

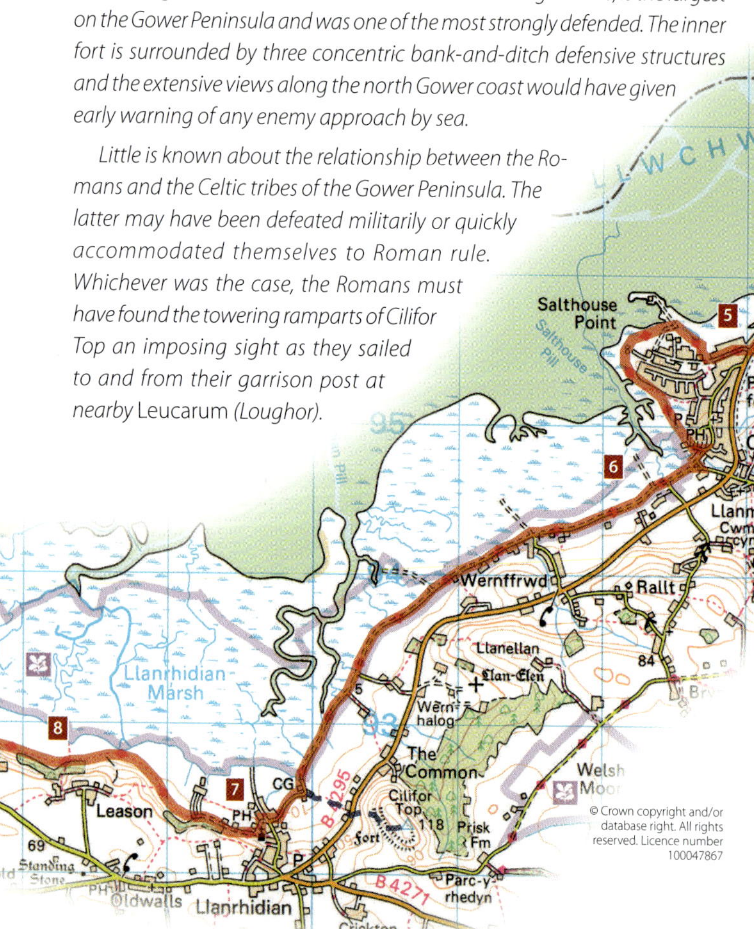

Wild and free?: *Semi-wild Gower ponies graze the open saltmarsh*

Shortly after passing below Cilifor Top, the road crosses a cattle grid and climbs gently between hedges (a footpath on the left emerges on the **B4295** opposite a permissive path to the fort). Reach a junction of lanes at the bottom of the village.

(The 'Welcome to Town' restaurant is further up the road, while buses to Pen-clawdd and Gowerton can be caught from the main road at the top of the village.)

7 Take the road on the right as you enter 👁 **Llanrhidian**. A few metres ahead, fork left (effectively straight on) past **Old Mill Cottage**. The road turns sharply left above a former **mill pond** and then sharp right onto a track signed to 'Weobley Castle and Landimore'. Bear left by **Stavel Hager Farm** ('Stáffal Haegr' on the OS Explorer map), crossing into fields and following the left-hand edge below steeply wooded slopes. Eventually, join an enclosed path between walls, with Weobley Castle clearly visible on the hilltop ahead.

8 The path now runs just inside the bottom edge of **Leason Wood**. After a kissing gate, bear left for a short distance uphill along a stony track and then turn right onto a narrow woodland path towards a gate into a long field. Follow the left-hand edge of the field until about halfway along, where a gate appears on the left. Join a path below trees, then cross a gravel track into a field and continue ahead along its left-hand edge.

Llanrhidian

A 'frontier' village on the north coast of Gower

Llanrhidian was historically the largest parish on the Gower Peninsula, extending along the north Gower coast from Weobley Castle to Pen-clawdd. The parish was divided by an invisible line separating the 'Englishry' of Llanrhidian Lower (the village of Llanrhidian itself) from the 'Welshry' of Llanrhidian Higher (the area around Pen-clawdd). The latter region was only thinly populated until the industrial developments of the post-medieval period.

In contrast to Pen-clawdd, Llanrhidian is a traditional rural village whose narrow, higgledy-piggledy streets and beautiful historic buildings create the feel of a place that time has passed by. Particularly beautiful is the Lower Mill, at the bottom end of the village. The small stream that once powered the mill tumbles down between houses and into the former mill pond.

Though peaceful today, Llanrhidian was at one time a 'frontier' village of Gower Anglicana and at the frontline of the struggle between native Welsh and their Anglo-Norman overlords. A remnant of these troubled times is the large masonry block built into the parapet of the parish church's massive tower. Known as the Parson's Bed, this block was used as a giant fireplace in which to create a warning beacon at times of imminent attack.

More information: The Swansea Bay website at www.visitswanseabay.com/destinations/gower-peninsula/ contains useful information about the Gower Peninsula.

Detour: *To visit Weobley Castle*

Just after entering the field, a signed path on the left leads up to 👁 **Weobley Castle** (pronounced *Web-lee*), a fortified manor house with spectacular views over **Llanrhidian Marsh**.

During the fourteenth century, the castle was home to the de la Bere family, but was lost early in the following century when it was attacked and severely damaged by the armies of Owain Glyndŵr. Much later, during the reign of Henry VII (1485–1509), the castle passed into the hands of another Welshman, Sir Rhys ap Thomas, a close ally of the king who had played an instrumental role in ensuring his victory at the Battle of Bosworth; he may even have been personally responsible for the death on the battlefield of Henry's rival, Richard III. It is Sir Rhys who was largely responsible for transforming the original Norman castle into the splendid manor house of today.

Unfortunately, Sir Rhys's labours were largely in vain, at least as far as his own family were concerned. In 1531, only six years after Sir Rhys's death, his grandson and heir, Rhys ap Gruffydd, was executed by Henry VIII for treason and his estates confiscated by the Crown. The castle is currently managed by Cadw and open to the public between April and October.

9 Go through a kissing gate and enter a long, narrow and sometimes boggy field. Head straight across the middle of the next field towards Landimore, passing through a kissing gate at the bottom end of a hedge. Bear right to a kissing gate, then follow waymarkers across a number of small fields to a road. Turn right down the hill.

Descend through **Landimore** village, passing the National Trust property of **Bovehill** on the left.

Detour: *To visit Bovehill Castle*
Don't miss ruined, overgrown 👁 **Bovehill Castle** on top of the hill near Bovehill Farm.

10 At the end of the road, continue onto a rough track along the edge of **Landimore Marsh**. After a little over 1 kilometre, this begins to curve left, passing below the spectacular rocky outcrop of **North Hill Tor**. After passing round a sharp left-hand bend and crossing a new bridge, follow **Burry Pill** upstream towards Llanmadoc.

'Pill' is a term common to both sides of the Bristol Channel and is generally used to describe a tidal stream or small river; its application to non-tidal parts of rivers is probably peculiar to Gower. The longest of Gower's pills, Burry Pill rises near the village of Burry and meanders north into a long tidal inlet between Whiteford Point and Landimore Marsh. Despite its modest size, the pill's waters played an important role in powering the local corn-milling industry, with no fewer than seven mills sited along its banks.

The Wales Coast Path skirts the spongy margins of Landimore Marsh

Wet or dry?: *The stepping stones across Burry Pill are covered at high tide*

11 With a hedge ahead, follow a sign for 'Cwm Ivy' to the right. If possible, cross Burry Pill by **stepping stones** and bear left towards a gate and signpost. The section ends here, with Llanmadoc signed up the track to the left. On reaching the road, the **Britannia Inn** is a short distance down to the left, while the main village is up the hill on the right.

Alternative route: *Avoiding the stepping stones*

At high water, the stepping stones are covered and it is not possible to cross Burry Pill on foot. If this is the case, retrace your steps for a short distance, then continue along an enclosed path up the hill ahead. This passes through a series of kissing gates and then along the right-hand edge of a field. Go through a gate onto a second enclosed path and turn right to reach a road junction. Continue down the hill into **Cheriton** and round a right-hand bend. The Coast Path can be rejoined by taking the first signed footpath on the right, not far beyond the Britannia Inn.

Llanmadoc to Rhossili

Distance: *10 miles / 17 kilometres (distances for longer route via Whiteford Point)* |
Start: *Llanmadoc SS 447 936* **Finish:** *Rhossili SS 414 881* | **Maps:** *Ordnance Survey
Explorer 164, Landranger 159*

Outline: An incredibly varied section, combining marshland, dunes,
cliffs and forests — not to mention some of Gower's finest beaches.

From Llanmadoc, you follow an old sea wall across the marshes to Whiteford
Burrows and a choice of routes. The longer, recommended route crosses
dunes and marshland to Whiteford Point, then tracks back along the wild,
open beach of Whiteford Sands. Both routes rejoin to climb Hills Tor, a fabulous
vantage point between Whiteford and Broughton (at low tide you can round
the headland on the beach below). There is more delightful walking along
the sand dune cliffs between Broughton and Burry Holms, a tidal island at
the north end of Rhossili Bay. A superb sandy beach stretches all the way
from here to Rhossili.

Services: *Just off the route in Llanmadoc is the Britannia Inn. There are also B&Bs,
a bunkhouse, a campsite and a post office in Llanmadoc. Halfway along Rhossili Bay
at Hillend is a campsite, toilets and a café. Swansea TIC: 01792 468321 | tourism@
swansea.gov.uk. Swallow Travel: 01792 898888.*

👁 **Don't miss: Whiteford Point Lighthouse** – a historic cast-iron lighthouse
at the mouth of the Loughor Estuary | **Burry Holms** – small tidal island associ-
ated with St Cenydd | **The Beacon, Rhossili Down** – highest point on the Gower
Peninsula with stunning panoramic views

▲ *Whiteford Burrows and Cwm Ivy Tor*

Llanmadoc

Llanmadoc's name is derived from St Madoc, a sixth-century saint of possible Irish origin who was a pupil of St David and St Cenydd. Little is known about Madoc himself, but a Romano-Celtic inscription (c.AD500), now set into a window sill of the parish church, and two inscribed pillar stones from a century or two later, are evidence of early Christian worship in the area.

The present church — the smallest in Gower — is dedicated to Madoc and dates from the thirteenth century. The building was much restored during the 1860s, when the famous Gower historian and woodcarver, the Reverend J. D. Davies, was rector. Much of the carving in the church is Davies's own work, and it was Davies who uncovered and recorded traces of medieval wall paintings concealed during the Reformation.

Unlikely though it may seem, Llanmadoc also has a long history as a port. At high tide, limestone from quarries on the peninsula was transported by boat down the narrow, winding channel of Burry Pill, while coal and culm would be brought in from mines in Carmarthenshire. There were some thirty ships involved in the trade during its height in the 1830s and '40s.

A lone walker on the vast expanse of Whiteford Sands

Wildlife haven: *Dunes and forest at Whiteford National Nature Reserve, backed by Cwm Ivy Tor*

The route: **Llanmadoc to Rhossili**

1 From the centre of **Llanmadoc**, head east and take the lane on the left around 100 metres before the **Britannia Inn**. Keep right at a fork and follow the track that heads down towards the salt marsh.

Keep ahead where the path from the stepping stones over **Burry Pill** joins from the right, signed to 'Cwm Ivy'. Pass a **whitewashed cottage** to reach a kissing gate at the corner of **Cwm Ivy Woods**.

(The official route of the Wales Coast Path turns right and immediately left here along the sea wall. But the wall protecting Cwm Ivy Marsh has been breached flooding the area with saltwater. Work is ongoing to repair this storm damage to the sea-wall and the Coast Path has been temporarily re-routed; please follow the diversion via Cwm Ivy Woods.)

The embankment dates from the seventeenth century and was built to reclaim a section of Cwm Ivy Marsh from the sea. East of the wall, a vast salt marsh extends the entire length of the north Gower coast. This unreclaimed land is subject to regular incursions by the sea and is threaded by numerous tidal creeks. The largest of these, Burry Pill, was once navigable as far as the lower end of Llanmadoc village, where the remains of an old stone boathouse and a former harbour, now silted up, can be seen.

Temporary Diversion via Cwm Ivy Woods: Turn left along a path/track that follows the edge of **Cwm Ivy Woods** and past a **bird hide** overlooking **Cwm Ivy Marsh**. Less than a kilometre later, the track reaches the hamlet of **Cwm Ivy**. Turn left then sharp right almost immediately along the road between the houses and cottages. In around

Whiteford NNR

This low-lying peninsula, sandwiched between sea and estuary, is one of the most remote spots on Gower. There is a great variety of habitat here: dunes, beach, salt marsh, mud flats and woodland can all be found within the reserve's 3,000 acres. Wildfowl and waders overwinter in large numbers on the Loughor estuary, while rare butterflies and wildflowers enliven the dunes in spring and early summer.

250 metres the track swings right and a sandy track continues ahead towards the beach.

Alternative route: *A shorter way across Cwm Ivy*

At the east of Cwm Ivy Woods, follow the temporary diversion past the hamlet of Cwm Ivy onto the track heading northwest. The longer Coast Path option via Whiteford Point is rejoined in front of a metal gate leading towards **Whiteford Sands** and the sea. Do not go through this gate, but bear left along a grassy track to a wooden gate.

2 Around Whiteford Point: *(Longer option)*

From the diverted route heading north from the hamlet of **Cwm Ivy**, turn right at the signpost into 'Whiteford Burrows', past a **cottage** and on along the wooded edge of the sand dunes passing **Cwm Ivy Lodge Bunkhouse** (pleasantly located in a clearing in the sand dune forest). Beyond the woods (and where it rejoins the **official Wales Coast Path** route at the north side of the sea wall) a sandy track continues along the boundary between **Whiteford Burrows** and the salt marsh. As the track curves left, away from the marsh, bear slightly right onto a narrower path. This is marked as part of the **Wales Coast Path** and continues to follow the **marshland edge**. (If the official path is flooded, it is possible to carry on along the track, and join the Coast Path later.)

Where directed, bear slightly left, away from the marsh, and pass through conifers planted to stabilise the dunes. The path is well marked and emerges at an **information board** on the edge of a sandy beach facing the **Loughor estuary**. Keep ahead to a waymark post in the sand and follow the arrow left along the beach towards

👁 **Whiteford Point.**

Iron guardian: *Now disused, Whiteford Point Lighthouse is uniquely constructed of cast iron*

Detour: *To Whiteford lighthouse*

At low tide, it is possible to walk across the sand to the lighthouse. But beware of rapid incoming tides that can quickly surround you.

It's the only cast-iron lighthouse in Britain to be sited actually in the sea The lighthouse was built in 1865 and marks a particularly dangerous shoal lying just off Whiteford Point. Unfortunately, it was unable to prevent a major shipwreck in 1868, when a dozen vessels sailing from Llanelli were driven onto the sands off the Point by a heavy ground swell. Six were eventually refloated, the others wrecked, and fifteen crew members drowned.

3 Follow the beach around the headland and then along the length of **Whiteford Sands**. Where the high tide line begins to curve right, leave the beach and join a waymarked track in the direction of **Cwm Ivy Tor**. (At low tide, you also have the option of continuing along the beach below Hills Tor into Broughton Bay.) Follow a fence to a corner and then turn sharply left to reach a metal gate and junction to the right of conifers. Go through the gate and turn right onto a grassy track towards a wooden gate. You have now rejoined the shorter coast path route via Cwm Ivy.

Official route: Following Wales Coast Path signs, climb a steep sandy path to reach an open grassy area. Continue along a level cliff-top path to the end of the headland at **Hills Tor.** After enjoying the spectacular views along **Whiteford Sands** and across **Broughton Bay**, turn sharply left.

4 An obvious grassy path heads towards Broughton Bay, before turning inland towards a **caravan park**. Descend on a signed sandy path to the edge of the site and turn right. The path continues around the back of Broughton Bay, with dunes to the right.

Go past a field gate on the right, passing through a smaller gate just beyond it onto a sandy path through the dunes. (At this point, you may wish to turn right towards the sea and follow the beach to Broughton.) As you approach **Broughton Farm**, the sandy surface of the path is replaced by grass and a signed path to 'Llangennith' is passed on the left. Keep ahead and join a track to the right of a barn, heading towards the caravan site beyond. To the right is a pleasant grassy area with benches overlooking the beach.

5 Bear slightly left onto a road through the caravan park and follow it round to the left. As the road straightens, turn sharp right at a waymark post onto a short dead-end road between caravans. An obvious path continues ahead along the coast.

Follow Wales Coast Path waymarkers along the **boardwalk** up the hill, passing a footpath forking right to a stunning viewpoint above **Twlc Point**.

Burry Holms can be reached easily at low tide

Burry Holms

A long history of habitation on a small tidal island

If tide conditions allow, it is worth crossing the short causeway onto 👁 **Burry Holms** to see the remains of a small medieval hermitage dedicated to St Cenydd, a sixth-century saint also responsible for founding a church in Llangennith. Not much is known about St Cenydd, but he was probably a pupil of St Illtyd, whose monastery at Llanilltyd Fawr (Llantwit Major in its current English form) provided religious instruction for many early Welsh saints. Within the remains of the medieval building on Burry Holms, traces of a wooden oratory and walled enclosure have been found that may have been part of the original sixth-century building.

Some centuries prior to St Cenydd's occupation, Burry Holms was the site of an Iron Age fort; a defensive ditch, hacked out of the island's limestone, still clearly bisects the island from north to south. Much earlier still, Mesolithic hunters seem to have had a seasonal camp on what was then a small hill around 19km (12 miles) from the sea.

The current name of the island is Norse in origin, suggesting that Burry Holms may have been used as a base by Viking raiders. Vikings sacked the nearby village of Llangennith in 986, destroying the church dedicated to St Cenydd.

More information: Details of early Mesolithic finds on the island can be found at: www.dyfedarchaeology.org.uk

Running wild: *Children sprint over Rhossili Down with Worms Head silhouetted out to sea*

At the top, join a grassy path through the burrows to the cliffs above **Bluepool Corner**, where a sandy beach is visible at low tide.

This small bay is accessible only by foot at low tide and involves an awkward scramble at the bottom. The blue pool from which the bay gets its name is a circular rock pool some 15 feet in diameter and 8 feet deep. Because of its consistent depth and surrounding high rocks, the pool is a popular diving spot.

West of Bluepool Corner is the cave of **Culver Hole** *(not to be confused with the better known Culver Hole near Port-Eynon). The skeletal remains of over forty people have been found here alongside burial urns dating from the Bronze Age. The presence of Iron Age pottery, Roman coins and early medieval jewellery suggests continued usage over many centuries.*

6 Continue along the **cliffs** and shortly descend a grassy slope towards the tidal island of **Burry Holms**. Do not descend onto the stony causeway (unless crossing to the island), but bear left along a grassy path until it becomes possible to drop onto the long, sandy beach of **Rhossili Bay**.

The three-mile stretch of sand between Burry Holms and Worms Head is one of the most spectacular beaches in Britain. Backed by dunes in the north and **Rhossili Down** *in the south, the beach is naturally protected from any form of commercial development and endowed with a powerful sense of wild splendour.*

7 Follow the beach south as far as **Diles Lake**, a small stream draining Llangennith Moors. Continue past the stream for another 200 metres or so, then turn left onto a waymarked sandy path through the dunes. The Coast Path leaves the beach here to join the bridleway along the foot of **Rhossili Down**.

Alternative route: *Along the beach to Rhossili village*

If preferred, it is also possible to continue along the beach to its southern terminus below **Rhossili**. A long flight of steps climbs steeply from the beach, emerging in Rhossili alongside the **Worms Head Hotel**.

8 Continuing on the **official route**, turn right at a track, shortly reaching a car park. Follow the track left, up the hill, and keep ahead through **Hillend Camping & Caravan Park** to the main entrance. (Before reaching the entrance, you will pass a café and public toilets.) Turn right immediately after the entrance through a gate to the base of **Rhossili Down**.

Alternative route: *Along the top of Rhossili Down to Rhossili village*

Instead of following the path along the foot of the common, you may prefer to climb the steep, grassy slope ahead and follow the path over the **top of Rhossili Down**. *In clear, calm weather, the walk along the crest of the ridge is one of the finest on the Gower Peninsula; late summer and autumn, when the heather on the slopes of the Down glows russet, are particularly beautiful. Numerous ancient stones scattered across the hillside add to the walk's charm and testify to a human presence on the Down that extends back to the Neolithic (c.4000–2400 BC). Indeed, concealed in the heather on the Down's eastern slopes are the remains of two megalithic burial chambers built around 2500 BC. The structures were*

Sunlight and stormy skies cast a dramatic light over Rhossili Bay

Cloud cap: *Early morning cloud rolls off the top of Rhossili Down*

once thought to be the work of the Vikings and named **Sweyne's Howes** *after the legendary Norse founder of Swansea. On the west side of the ridge, facing the sea, a concrete level marks the site of a World War II gun emplacement, sited to prevent a German invasion along Rhossili Beach.*

The 193-metre summit of 👁 **The Beacon**, *at the southern end of the down, is the highest point on the Gower Peninsula and commands sweeping views of the Bristol Channel, Carmarthen Bay and down the peninsula towards Swansea. On a clear day it is possible to see Fan Brycheiniog in the Brecon Beacons, as well as the coasts of Pembrokeshire and Devon. The view of Worms Head and Rhossili Bay below is also superb.*

9 To keep to the **official route,** follow the path to the right, along the base of the common. Initially, views towards the sea are blocked by the caravan site, but shortly improve. The path is used by horses, so you may need to climb slightly higher up the slope to avoid any muddy sections. Pass behind the iconic, white-painted **Old Rectory** (said to be Britain's most sought after rental property owned by the National Trust) and climb to a gate at the southern end of the down. You are rejoined at this point by the alternative route over the top of Rhossili Down.

10   Follow a broad track ahead as far as **St Mary's Church**. Turn right here, following a Wales Coast Path sign along an enclosed path to the side of the churchyard. Emerge in a bus turning area and follow the road downhill to a large **car park** opposite the **Bay Bistro** and the **Worms Head Hotel.** There are also a number of other snack and gift shops, and toilets at the bottom of the car park.

The Old Rectory, Rhossili

Built in the 1850s, The Old Rectory replaced an older building used by smugglers, and was home for over 40 years to the Reverend John Ponsonby Lucas. Local legend says the rector's ghostly steed can still be heard galloping across the sands between Rhossili and Llangennith. Such apparitions have not deterred visitors, The Old Rectory today being one of the National Trust's most sought-after rental properties.

Rhossili to Oxwich

Distance: *12 miles / 19 kilometres*| **Start:** *Rhossili SS 414 881*| **Finish:** *Oxwich SS 500 864* | **Maps:** *Ordnance Survey Explorer 164, Landranger 159*

Outline: This section explores the Gower Peninsula's rugged south coast and contains some of the finest sections of coastal walking in the country.

From Rhossili, the Wales Coast Path descends gently towards the dramatic promontory of Worms Head — well worth walking out to if the tide permits. Heading east, the path then crosses a series of grassy clifftops punctuated by narrow, steep-sided valleys. As far as Port-Eynon, the cliffs are characterised by some magnificent limestone formations. Past Port-Eynon Bay, the path continues below low, limestone cliffs as far as Oxwich Point, where you enter Oxwich National Nature Reserve. A strip of beautiful coastal woodland clings to the steep, sheltered slopes above Oxwich Bay, but be prepared for steps — lots of them!

Services: *There's a range of accommodation types, including campsites and hostels, in Rhossili and Port-Eynon, as well as toilets, pubs, cafés and fish and chip shops. There is also a post office in Port-Eynon. Swansea TIC: 01792 468321 | tourism@swansea.gov. uk. Data Cabs: 01792 474747*

Don't miss: Worms Head – iconic tidal headland at Gower's 'Land's End' **Mewslade Bay** – lovely sandy beach below spectacular limestone cliffs | **Culver Hole** – peculiar walled-up cave once serving as a dovecote

▲ *Worms Head juts almost a mile out to sea*

Rhossili

Although the name **Rhossili** is Welsh in origin, the village became part of English-speaking Gower following the Norman conquest of the peninsula in the twelfth century and was settled extensively from the west of England. In the troubled centuries that followed, the village, like others in Gower Anglicana, remained vulnerable to raids from its hostile Welsh neighbours. As a result, St Mary's, like many Gower churches built in the twelfth and thirteenth centuries, was provided with a strong tower that could act as a place of refuge during times of warfare and raiding.

Interestingly, the original pre-Norman village was located close to the beach, on a strip of land known as 'The Warren'. Storms during the thirteenth century 'besanded' the village, forcing its inhabitants to rebuild on the cliffs above. The original Rhossili was never forgotten by villagers, but it was only following a storm and archaeological dig in 1979–80 that conclusive evidence of its existence was uncovered. There is information on the dig and its discoveries in St Mary's Church, as well as a memorial to Petty Officer Edgar Evans, a naval officer who was born in Rhossili and died on Captain Scott's ill-fated expedition to the South Pole in 1912.

The gaunt ribs of the 'Helvetia' with Worms Head on the horizon

Dragon's head?: *A group of walkers pause to take in the clifftop views of Worms Head*

The route: **Rhossili to Oxwich**

1 From the **National Trust car park**, follow the well-surfaced track past the **visitor centre** towards Worms Head.

As you leave **Rhossili village,** *there are stunning views along the full length of Rhossili Bay. Study the sand carefully at low tide and you will also be able to make out the remains of a ship, the Helvetia, which foundered in November 1887. Before modern navigational equipment, the jagged rocks of Worms Head made the coast near Rhossili particularly dangerous to shipping: over thirty wrecks have been identified in Rhossili Bay, most from the late nineteenth and early twentieth centuries.*

The main Wales Coast Path bears left at the end of a stone wall.

Alternative route: *via the old coastguard's lookout*

It's worth continuing ahead along a grassy track to the **old coast- guards' lookout** building overlooking Worms Head. *This former coastguard station is now an information point manned by Coastwatch volunteers.* **Caution:** *A sign outside publicises the safe crossing times to Worms Head each day. To the north-west is a small bay called* **Kitchen**

Corner *where limestone quarried from the coastal cliffs was once loaded onto ships.* From the lookout station, turn left along the top of the cliffs to rejoin the main Coast Path alongside a dry-stone wall.

Detour: *To the far end of Worms Head, depending on the tide*
Crossing to 'The Worm' (as the headland is known locally) is possible for around two and a half hours either side of low tide. These times are

Gower's Land's End

Worms Head's *narrow promontory is one of Gower's iconic attractions. Its name comes from the Old English word for dragon and describes the headland's silhouette: three high backs and a slender neck. Now a nature reserve, the headland is connected to the mainland by a rocky causeway for 2½ hours at low tide. The end is two kilometres away, and crossing can take far longer than expected.*

usually on display outside the coastguard lookout station. Be aware that there is no clear path across the rocky, uneven channel, and that the crossing can take much longer than expected.

A path of over a kilometre in length connects the Inner Head with the Outer Head (it is possible to go around or over the top of the first). Most of this is easy to follow, with the exception of a short, rocky scramble at the far end of the Inner Head, which some may find difficult. The way to the Outer Head then continues across a narrow isthmus and over a spectacular sea arch known as Devil's Bridge. There are great views from the raised promontory at the far end of the headland, but if determined to go all the way, make sure you've allowed plenty of time to get back safely.

The **official route** stays with the wall as it descends towards **Tears Point**, before turning sharply left at a corner. Take the upper, left-hand path ahead and continue along the cliffs above **Fall Bay**.

2 Near an access path to the beach, the waymarked path curves right below a small cliff face, then bears back to the left to continue above **Mewslade Bay**. At a wall corner, with jagged limestone crags and pinnacles ahead, the path bears left again, following a dry-stone wall.

Alternative route: *A narrow, exposed path above Mewslade Bay*
At this point, those with a head for heights may wish to bear right, onto an unsigned footpath that follows a spectacular but vertiginous route along a rocky ledge and around the back of Mewslade Bay. However, this narrow, exposed path will not be to everyone's taste

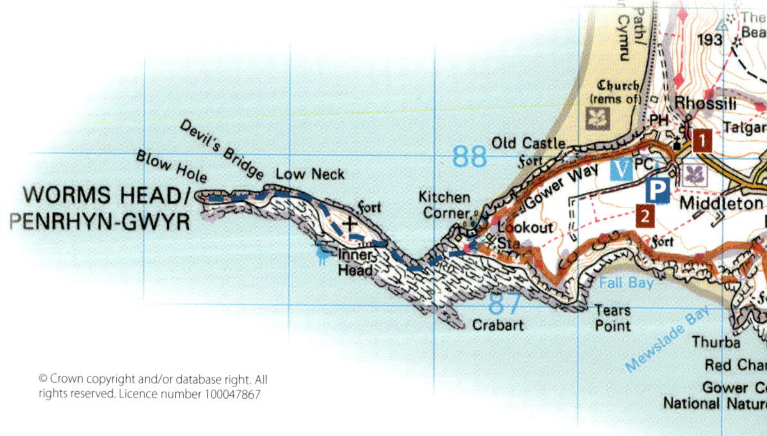

Early etching showing the excavation at 'Goat Hole', Paviland

The 'Red Lady of Paviland'

The discovery of Britain's oldest modern human

In 1823, Oxford University's first professor of geology, the Reverend William Buckland, stumbled across the partial remains of a human skeleton in a small cave between Port-Eynon and Rhossili. The bones were stained with red ochre and there was jewellery made from shells and ivory close by. Concluding that the remains were female, the reverend speculated that the woman had been a prostitute and was connected to the Iron Age fort on the cliffs a short distance above the cave.

The reverend was wrong on at least two counts. 'The Red Lady of Paviland' was not only a young man, he was also considerably older than the reverend dared contemplate — the most recent carbon dating techniques have suggested a figure of 34,000 years. Sea level at that time was some 80 metres lower than today and the cave would have been located on the edge of a large tundra plain stretching south towards Exmoor.

Though Paviland's 'Red Lady' was by no means the first person to set foot in Gower — flint tools used by Neanderthal people 70,000 years ago have also been discovered in the cave — he is nonetheless, and by a considerable margin, the first known human in Britain to belong indisputably to our species.

More information: An evocative article on Paviland's 'Red Lady' can be found in Nigel Jenkins & David Pearl, *Gower* (Gomer Press, 2009), pp. 50–6.

Limestone and salt: *A walker approaches Port-Eynon with its limestone platforms and old salt house*

and is certainly not suitable for young children. If you do choose this option, return to the main Coast Path by following the narrow **Mew Slade valley** inland until a signed cross-path is reached.

On the **official route**, watch out for a path on the right, in a dip, that descends steeply into narrow **Mew Slade valley**. Drop to a grassy track running along the bottom of the valley (turning right here will take you down to 👁 **Mewslade Bay**) and go through a kissing gate in the wall ahead.

3 Climb steeply out of the valley and continue ahead along a grassy cliff-top path, soon joining the line of a wall. After a gate, stay close to the wall as it begins to curve left, then follow the path descending steeply into another narrow, steep-sided valley. Reach a cross-path at the bottom, signed to 'Pitton' on the left and **Ram Grove** (the rocky coastal inlet below) on the right. Continue ahead on a narrow path climbing out of the valley.

After climbing steeply through thick undergrowth, the path once more continues along a level, grassy cliff top, heading seawards towards the earthworks of an **Iron Age promontory fort**. After passing through a gate amid the ramparts, bear left until a clear path is picked up. Pass behind the back

of a shallow valley to another gate, then continue between gorse bushes until the path emerges back out in the open. At a fork, take the main path directly ahead to reach a gap in a wall, then a gate. More level grassy walking leads into another steep, narrow valley, **Foxhole Slade**. Go through the metal gate at the bottom to reach a junction of paths. The Coast Path continues straight ahead, while a path alongside the wall on the right leads down to the coast near **Paviland Cave**.

Dovecote or hideout?

Culver Hole is one of Gower's oddities. Both its name (*culver* is an old term for a pigeon) and the tiers of nest boxes inside suggest this walled-up cave was once a dovecote belonging to the long-gone Port-Eynon Castle. Yet the floors and staircase inside seem inconsistent with its use solely as a dovecote, and it's been suggested that the cave was later used as a smugglers' hideout.

Detour: *To Paviland Cave*

Paviland Cave is only safely accessible at low tide, when a sandy spit at the bottom of Foxhole Slade allows access to the bottom of a steep shoulder of rock to the right. A relatively easy scramble leads up to the cave. (An alternative path, along the side of the cliff above, is extremely hairy and not recommended.) *There is not a great deal to see in the cave; its significance derives entirely from the discovery here in 1823 of a prehistoric human skeleton, the erroneously named 'Red Lady' (see interpretation on page 161).*

4 Climb steeply out of the narrow valley and back onto the grassy cliffs. Continue across the **common** for a further 1.5 kilometres, until you reach a metal field gate across the path. Do not go through, but take the obvious path bearing right, towards the sea, alongside a drystone wall. Eventually, this curves back inland, rejoining the main track. Turn right and descend gently between hedges. At the bottom of the dip, take the path on the right, back towards the coast.

5 Descend along a **pretty limestone valley** to the sea. Turn left through a gate

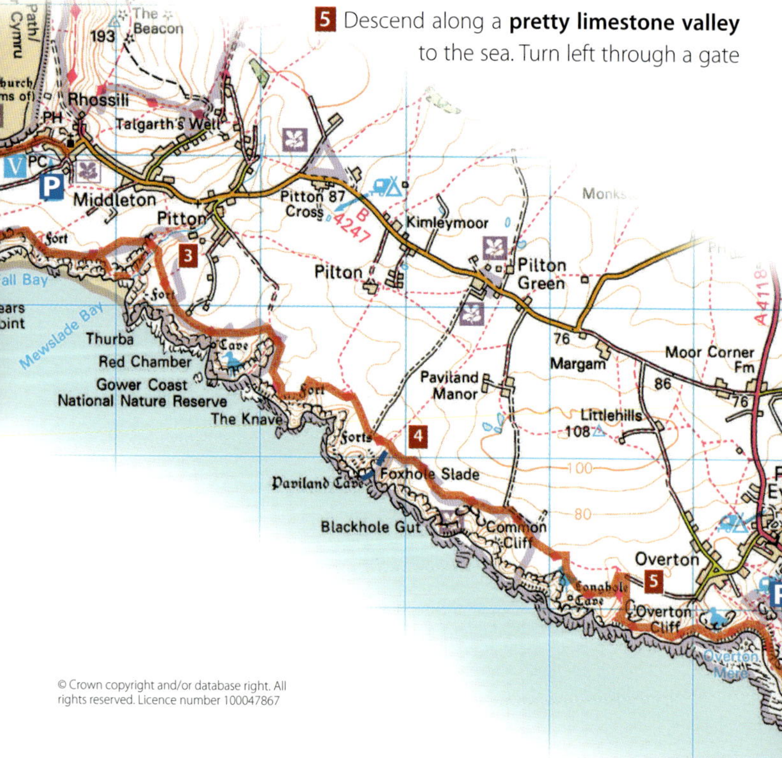

Limestone ledges: *Low limestone cliffs and flat rock platforms in Port-Eynon Bay*

and follow a narrow, undulating path, which hugs the coast below limestone crags. Continue around the back of **Overton Mere** as far as an obvious path climbing steeply up the slope of the headland on the left.

Sea castle: *Oxwich Castle overlooks the long curve of Oxwich Bay*

Detour: *To mysterious Culver Hole*

A short path between the bottom of the slope and the sea leads to a deep rocky fissure containing one of Gower's most intriguing caves, **Culver Hole**. *Local legend claims there's a secret tunnel linking the cave with the salt house on the far side of Port-Eynon Point.*

To continue on the **official route**, at the top of the climb keep ahead across the exposed headland towards a **granite memorial** to two founder members of the Gower Society, Gwent Jones and Stephen Lee. Turn left at the memorial, aiming towards a **derelict salt house** on the rocky shores of **Port-Eynon Bay** below.

Prior to refrigeration, salt was a highly valued commodity, being the only means of preserving meat, and a coastal village like Port-Eynon provided an ideal location for extracting salt from sea water. Typically, water from the sea would be collected in large, shallow, open pans and then heated (initially by burning wood and at a later date coal) until salt crystals had formed. These would be raked out and more sea water added. The scale and sophistication of the industry in Port-Eynon is impressive and suggests that the village was a major trader in salt during the medieval and early modern periods.

6 Join a slippery path descending diagonally left through debris from what was once a major limestone quarry. Pass between hedges and, at a fork straight after, take the path on the left (or fork right to continue down to the salt house and a permissive path through the campsite on the left). Continue through woodland to a junction, where you turn right and descend towards the sea. Cross a campsite access track and emerge on the beach by a **youth hostel**. Turn left along the top of the beach, passing a slipway. The coast path continues around the beach to Horton, but at the next gap, there is an exit off the beach into the centre of **Port-Eynon**, where there are toilets, a pub, and a number of cafés and takeaways.

The Wales Coast Path continues along the beach, crossing a small stream and passing the access to the **RNLI station** before leaving the beach. It then climbs a flight of steps and turns right onto a track.

At the end of the track, continue onto a narrow path between hedges, signed 'Oxwich 3½'. A section of lovely coastal walking follows, along a mainly level path close to the sea below low-lying limestone cliffs.

7 Unfortunately, the line of the original path has eroded and collapsed, and you are soon forced to take a signed inland diversion around the back of fields. The path returns to the coast just above '**The Sands**', where at low tide a fine sandy beach is exposed. (The rope down a near-vertical bank may put some beach lovers off, but there is easier access at the farther end of the bay.)

After returning to the coast, the path is initially enclosed between the shore and a fence, but later runs across a wide, grassy area between low cliffs and the sea. As you approach **Oxwich Point**, the cliffs become more spectacular and views open up along the coast ahead towards Swansea. At a junction, bear right, following a Coast Path sign for 'Oxwich Point'. Continue round the headland, with Oxwich Bay, Tor Bay and Three Cliffs Bay all becoming visible ahead. Pass through a kissing gate into **Oxwich National Nature Reserve** and shortly enter **Oxwich Wood**.

8 Continue along the lower edge of the wood for around 500 metres before following the path left, up a long, steep hill. At the top, turn right along the upper woodland edge before dropping slightly to a signed fork. Take the right-hand path, marked 'Coast Path' and 'Oxwich Beach', and descend a long flight of steps to the sea.

Turn left at the bottom, past **St Illtyd's Church**, and continue along a lane to the **Oxwich Bay Hotel**. Access to the beach and a large car park is possible past public toilets on the right, but the official route continues along the road to a crossroads at the bottom end of the village.

Oxwich to Caswell Bay

Distance: *9 miles / 14 kilometres* | **Start:** *Oxwich SS 500 864* | **Finish:** *Caswell Bay SS 593 877* | **Maps:** *Ordnance Survey Explorer 164, Landranger 159*

Outline: This is another great section of coastal walking, containing dunes, dramatic limestone cliffs and several beautiful beaches.

The first half of the section, between Oxwich and Southgate, is dominated by dunes and sandy beaches. Dramatic limestone cliffs add another element to the mix, their high tops providing stunning views across Oxwich Bay and Three Cliffs Bay. Beyond Pennard Pill, high, grassy cliffs lead east past Southgate as far as Pwlldu Head, where there are far-reaching views along the south Gower coast. After a steep descent into Pwlldu Bay, you join a narrow, winding path through more rugged coastal scenery, finally dropping onto the popular sandy beach of Caswell.

Services: *There's a pub, toilets, cafés and a general store in Oxwich, as well as B&Bs, a hotel and a campsite. Southgate has a café, shop, toilets, a post office, B&Bs and a pharmacy. Swansea TIC: 01792 468321 | tourism@swansea.gov.uk. Data Cabs: 01792 474747*

Don't miss: **Great Tor** – grassy headland with a stunning view across Oxwich Bay | **Pennard Castle** – Norman ruin with spectacular views over Three Cliffs Bay | **Pwlldu Bay** – beautiful shingle and sand cove with links to the limestone industry

▲ *Iconic Three Cliffs Bay, on the Gower*

Oxwich

A distinct cluster of motte-and-bailey castles around Oxwich Bay — there are castles at Penmaen, Penrice and Oxwich itself — suggests that the area acted as a beachhead for the Norman invasion of the peninsula in the twelfth century. After conquering an area, the Normans typically erected such crude earth and timber structures, only later replacing them with stronger stone fortifications.

As elsewhere along the south Gower coast, Oxwich was 'ethnically cleansed' by its Norman occupiers, the original Welsh population being replaced by a layer of English peasantry. St Illtyd, to whom the parish church is dedicated, is one of the few reminders of the village's Celtic past.

The original Norman stronghold in Oxwich, sited on the high ground to the south of the village, was later replaced by a stone castle and then, in the sixteenth century, by a castellated manor house. This was home to the Mansel family, a powerful Gower clan who owned a number of substantial properties on the peninsula and a great deal of land. In addition to their legitimate activities, they were also deeply involved in the local smuggling and wrecking 'industries'. A more reputable inhabitant was the Methodist preacher John Wesley, who lived in the village between 1762 and 1773.

Great Tor seen from the dunes at the far end of Oxwich beach

The route: **Oxwich to Caswell Bay**

1 From the crossroads in **Oxwich**, take the road signed 'Swansea'. Taking care, stay on the righthand side of the road for a short distance before turning right at the signpost into **Oxwich National Nature Reserve.**

After leaving Oxwich, the Wales Coast Path passes through **Oxwich Burrows**, an area of national significance in terms of flora and fauna, but out of sight and sound of the sea. The soft, sandy paths of the burrows can also be hard going, too.

Alternative route: *Along the beach*

You may prefer to follow the beach from opposite the **Oxwich Bay Hotel** as far as **Nicholaston Pill**. A bridge across the pill a short distance upstream is currently closed for 'Health and Safety reasons', but, in warm weather, the shallow waters can be easily paddled.

Which route you choose after Nicholaston Pill may depend on the tide. Under most tidal conditions, you will be able to continue along the beach at least as far as **Tor Bay**, so avoiding more difficult walking through the loose sand of **Nicholaston Burrows.** A well-used path from Tor Bay can be used to rejoin the Coast Path as it passes around the edge of **Penmaen Burrows**, or, if the tide is right out, you can continue around **Great Tor** along the beach to **Three Cliffs Bay**. Either follow the base of the cliffs left, rejoining the Coast Path below the stepping stones across **Pennard Pill**, or paddle across the stream

Sand and sea: *The long curve of Oxwich Bay and its backing dunes seen from the air*

to **Pobbles Beach** and rejoin the official Coast Path as it climbs out of **Pennard Burrows**.

Back on the **official route**, the Wales Coast Path remains close to the road as far as a fork near a wooden nature reserve sign. Take the right-hand path, which passes to the right of the sign, and continue along the right-hand side of a fence. Frequent waymarkers guide you through an attractive dune

Tor bay?: *The view from the top of Great Tor, looking back towards Oxwich Bay*

landscape, though out of sight of the sea. Where the sea finally becomes visible once more, follow the arrow half left (the exact path is not immediately clear). Keep ahead and you should soon arrive at a **footbridge** across **Nicholaston Pill.**

2 Cross the bridge and keep straight ahead through **Nicholaston Burrows**. After passing below a rocky cliff face, watch out for a left fork into Nicholaston Woods. On emerging into an open area, with dunes to the right, bear left on to a path heading back into trees. Following waymarks closely, climb through woodland to the right of a stream. Where directed, turn right on to a more level path, still within trees and shortly with a fence to your left.

Eventually, the trees are left behind and the path emerges onto an open **headland** with excellent views of Oxwich Bay to the right. Continue along the cliff-top path, passing through a National Trust gate towards Tor Bay (the small cove between Little Tor and Great Tor). Follow the path around the back of the bay and along the top of the cliffs to 👁 **Great Tor**, an impressive grassy promontory separating Oxwich Bay from Three Cliffs Bay. After admiring the views along the length of the former, continue along the cliff-top path, which now bears round to the left above **Three Cliffs Bay**.

3 Stick to the main path as it bears left, away from the sea. You appear to be heading in the wrong direction, but will soon reach a signpost in an open area directing you to the right, down a steep sandy path. Follow the main path down to a **marshy area behind Three Cliffs Bay**. Bear left to a **boardwalk** and a path around the back of the marsh. Climb through trees, then shortly turn right along a waymarked path just above the edge of the tidal limit. Just after a path joins the main route from the left, drop down to **Pennard Pill** on the right and cross over **stepping stones**.

Once on the other side, keep ahead along a stony bar across the bay towards the steep, sandy slopes of **Pennard Burrows**. At the end of the bar at the base of the cliff, turn left at the signpost and then bear right at the next signpost to head up the slope. At the top, take a sharp right and follow the sandy path towards the Three Cliffs.

Ruined Pennard Castle dominates Pennard Burrows

Iconic bay: *Three Cliffs Bay is probably one of Gower's most beautiful beaches*

Detour: *To the ruins of Pennard Castle*

There is a good path to the ruins of 👁 **Pennard Castle**, about 600 metres over to the left. Return to this point to continue.

This dramatic ruin was probably built in the late thirteenth century to replace an earlier ringwork defence. Commanding views to the north and west seemed to provide an ideal location for a castle, but the building's Norman lords could not have foreseen the problem of encroaching sand, which destroyed the fertility of the surrounding land and forced them to abandon the castle by the end of the fourteenth century. The views across Three Cliffs Bay from the area of the castle are frequently cited as being among the best in Britain.

4 A sandy path follows a course high above **Three Cliffs Bay**, then descends along a path made of wooden slats into a shallow, sandy valley to the left of **Pobbles Beach**. Climb up the far slope of the valley on a steep, sandy path that later turns to grass. Near the top, bear left onto one of the many paths across the grassy cliff top to meet a lane in front of houses. Follow the road as far as a sharp left-hand bend by a car park. The Coast Path continues

straight ahead, along a grassy path on the seaward side of the car park. Just up the road to the left are toilets, a bus stop, and a combined general store and coffee shop called Pennard Stores.

The names **Pennard** *and* **Southgate** *are often used interchangeably, with most people referring to Southgate as Pennard. The original medieval settlement lay to the north-west, around* **Pennard Castle***, but was abandoned in*

Gower's choughs

The chough is a rare, crow-like bird with a distinctive red bill and legs. It is typically found on rocky western coasts, where it uses its curved bill to probe for insects. Until the 1990s, choughs had been absent from Gower for a century, but they have recently re-established two breeding colonies at Rhossili and Pennard. Watch and listen for their tumbling, acrobatic aerial displays and distinctive 'kee-aw' call.

Rock port: *Pwlldu Bay was once busy with ships exporting limestone from a local quarry*

1532 due to encroaching sand dunes. The village then found a new centre at St Mary's Church, some 2 kilometres to the east. Suburbanisation in the twentieth century led to the development of a new locus of settlement around Southgate. Fortunately, Pennard's stunning sea cliffs remain unspoilt and offer some of the finest coastal walking on Gower. Keep an eye out for choughs on this stretch.

5 From **Southgate**, continue eastwards along a wide grassy path running roughly parallel to a lane on the left. Briefly join the lane near **Hunts Farm** and then turn right almost immediately onto a path signed to 'Pwlldu Head'.

Continue along a grassy path across open cliffs. Follow waymarkers out to the far end of the headland, enjoying stunning views back along the coast towards Pennard Cliffs.

During the eighteenth century, it was common for the Royal Navy to acquire recruits through the use of 'press gangs'. In 1760, a naval ship called the Caesar was wrecked off Pwlldu Head, drowning 68 Swansea men who had been forced into the service. To prevent escape, the men had been imprisoned and probably shackled below deck. Their bodies were later buried by local villagers, who marked the mass grave — still known as Graves End — with a circle of limestone rocks.

6 From **Pwlldu Head**, bear left to join a stepped path descending steeply to the north-east. At the bottom of the slope, keep ahead to a waymark post, then follow the arrow steeply uphill to the left. Go through a gate and continue between hedges, the path soon levelling off near a good view of Pwlldu Bay on the right. Keep ahead through fields and a small copse to reach a junction with a track near **Pennard Farm**.

Bear right at the track, following a sign for 'Pwlldu Bay'. Descend quite sharply to an entrance gate to a house. Do not go through, but turn right onto a narrower path. Descend steeply on a rough, tree-lined bridleway to a small group of houses at the back of 👁 **Pwlldu Bay**. Turn right to visit the beach or left to continue along the Coast Path — the path can also be rejoined by crossing the beach to the far side of the bay.

7 A bit further along, bear left off the track to cross a footbridge over **Bishopston Pill.** Rejoin the gravel track on the far side of a **ford** and continue around the back of the bay. As the track starts to climb, turn right onto a path. This lovely, undulating trail hugs the coast closely for the next 1 kilometre/ 0.5 miles or so to **Brandy Cove**.

As well as being the haunt of smugglers, Brandy Cove was also used for the legitimate purpose of loading ore from nearby lead mines onto small boats.

Important: Before proceeding along the Coast Path to Caswell Bay, check the tide here; if the tide covers the beach at this point, please use the alternative high-tide route signposted from here and heading up the valley. Follow this route and at the top of the valley turn right, up steps and along the fields. Then turn right where the route joins the main road down into Caswell Bay. Take care, as there is no pavement and in holiday periods the road can get quite busy.

8 From **Brandy Cove**, continue to wind your way along the coast, passing round an exposed headland above **Caswell Bay**. Your route to the section finish in Caswell Bay is now tide dependent. Unless the tide is right in, turn right down a flight of steps and cross the sandy beach to where a small stream flows onto the sand. Cross by a culvert to avoid wet feet and leave the beach alongside various cafés and takeaways. There are public toilets across the road, as well as a car park and bus stop.

If the tide is in at the small headland ahead, take care and cross the pebble beach until you reach a path with a handrail, which leads up to the main road and a short section without pavement into Caswell Bay.

Caswell Bay to Swansea Marina

Distance: *9 miles / 15 kilometres* | **Start:** *Caswell Bay SS 593 877*
Finish: *Trafalgar Bridge, Swansea Marina SS 663 924* | **Maps:** *Ordnance Survey 164 & 165, Landranger 159*

Outline: A largely urban section through rugged coastal scenery to Mumbles Head, then round the long arc of Swansea Bay.

From Caswell Bay, the Wales Coast Path continues along an undulating but surfaced path across the cliffs to Langland, where it joins the promenade around Langland Bay. More rugged coastal scenery leads to Limeslade Bay, where you join a road to Mumbles Head. After descending steps to the pier, you join the Swansea Bay cycle path, which traces the arc of the bay to Swansea Marina (or you can walk along the beach). The section ends at the Trafalgar Bridge, a pedestrian and cyclist bridge just below the River Tawe Barrage.

Services: *There are pubs, cafés, takeaways, shops and toilets throughout this section, which is never far from an urban area. There are also B&Bs and hotels in Langland, Mumbles and Swansea, as well as banks, cash points, post offices and pharmacies in Mumbles and Swansea. Swansea TIC: 01792 468321 | tourism@swansea.gov.uk. Data Cabs: 01792 474747*

👁 **Don't miss: Mumbles Pier** – Victorian pier close to Mumbles Head | **Oystermouth Castle** – one of the largest and prettiest of Gower's castles | **National Waterfront Museum** – innovative museum telling the story of Wales's industrial and maritime heritage

▲ *Mumbles lighthouse and pier*

Caswell Bay

Along with a few Roman coins, the remains of an Iron Age promontory fort are the only real evidence of past habitation at **Caswell Bay**. In the latter part of the nineteenth century, a windmill was erected near the site of the fort to pump water from a well at the foot of the cliffs. After falling into disuse around 1900, the windmill continued to act as a popular landmark until it was destroyed by fire in 1930.

It was around this time that Caswell Bay's popularity as a holiday resort took off. After World War I, the boundaries of Swansea Borough had been extended to include the Mumbles and the south Gower coast as far as Caswell. The borough council set about widening and improving the narrow Coast Path between Mumbles Head and Caswell Bay, creating a popular walking route. At the same time, new housing developments began to extend west along the coast.

Fortunately, the high cliffs surrounding Caswell Bay have protected it from the worst features of development. Behind the bay is a wooded valley (Bishop's Wood Nature Reserve) popular with walkers and horse riders. The path through the valley ends at the ruins of an early Celtic chapel with a well and spring.

Caswell Bay from the air

The route: Caswell Bay to Swansea Marina

1 From **Caswell Bay**, join the well-used concrete path to Langland behind the cafés. The path climbs steeply over the headland called **Whiteshell Point** at the eastern end of the bay, then follows an undulating route below **Newton Cliff** to **Snaple Point**, at the western corner of **Langland Bay**.

2 Follow the popular **promenade** around the bay, passing some interesting-looking beach huts, as well as toilets and cafés. Climb slightly above a rocky area on the beach, then drop to a second sandy area at **Rotherslade** in front of the **Surfside Café**. Once past the café, stay with the concrete path as it winds its way along the beautiful Gower coast towards Mumbles Head.

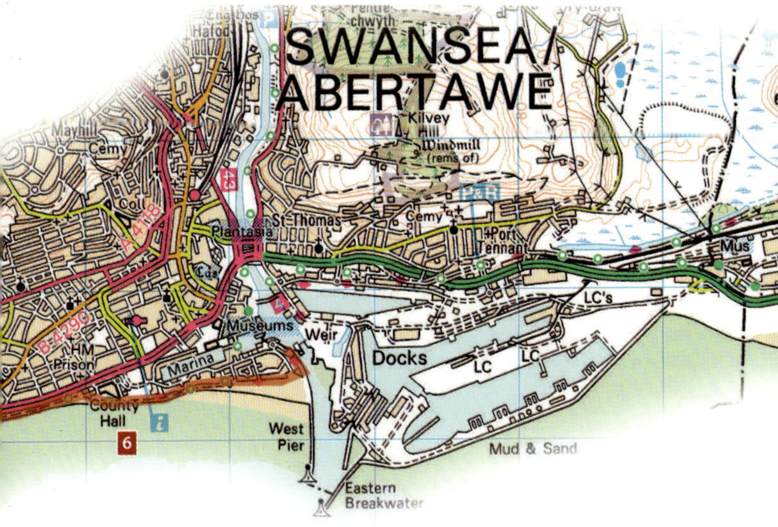

3 The path eventually emerges at a road in **Limeslade**, near Forte's café and ice cream parlour. Keep ahead along the pavement, following the road as it curves to the right. Pass car parks to your right (there are toilets and a café bar here), then, at a sharp left-hand bend, keep straight ahead to the back of a small car park above **Mumbles Head**. Steps at the back of the car park lead down to the **Mumbles** and the start of the long, curving arc of **Swansea Bay.**

At the bottom of the steps, turn right to see 👁 **Mumbles pier**. Otherwise, follow the car park access road left, as far as some metal bollards on the right. Go through the bollards and cross to the seaward side of a boat park. At the end of the boat-parking area, keep to the right of Verdi's café, shortly joining the start of the **Swansea Bay cycle path**.

4 Navigation is now simple, as you follow the cycle path around the long curve of Swansea Bay, between the sea and the main road to your left. The only thing to watch out for are fast-moving cyclists!

Detour: *A visit to a nearby ruined castle*

Less than 2 kilometres from the pier, it's worth a short detour to the left to visit 👁 **Oystermouth Castle**.

As you walk towards Swansea, there are a number of pubs and cafés which

(Continued on page 184)

Dawn mists obscure Mumbles lighthouse

The Mumbles

A characterful village on the edge of Swansea

There are competing explanations for the origins of the name Mumbles, though almost everyone agrees it referred originally to the two islands now known as Mumbles Head. The name may derive from the verb 'to mumble' and refer to the sound of the sea on the headland's rocks, or it could come from the French or Latin for breasts and describe the shape of the two islands when viewed from sea. A French origin would suggest that the name dates from the time of the Normans, whose castle at nearby Oystermouth dominated the area for several centuries.

By the end of the eighteenth century, a lighthouse had been constructed on the outer of the Mumbles' two islands and a village of narrow, densely packed streets had developed on the steeply rising slopes between the sea and Mumbles Hill. Although the dominant industry was fishing, the developing

Mumbles pier

coal industry in the nearby Clyne Valley was becoming increasingly important. In 1804, a railway track was laid around the edge of Swansea Bay, connecting the Mumbles with both Swansea and the Clyne Valley; three years later, the railway's horse-drawn carriages were carrying the first tourists to the village as well as wagons of coal for export. Unlike a tramline, the track was set apart from any road, making it the first passenger railway in the world.

Competition from horse-drawn buses put an end to rail passenger services for two-and-a-half decades from 1830. However, the introduction of steam engines in 1877 marked the beginning of a golden era in the history of the railway line. From 1898, passengers were unloaded directly onto the end of the newly opened Mumbles Pier, and by the first decade of the twentieth century the line was carrying as many as 40,000 passengers on bank holidays. The railway continued to prosper until after World War Two, when the spread of car ownership led to an inevitable decline culminating in the line's final closure in 1960.

Mumbles lighthouse

Now a popular pedestrian and cycle path, the route of the former railway continues to bring visitors into Mumbles. In recent years, the village has also cultivated a well-earned reputation for the number and quality of its restaurants. To the relief of local residents, the development of Swansea's Wind Street has more or less killed off 'The Mumbles Mile': a regular Saturday-night pub crawl between the promenade's numerous public houses.

> *"Mumbles is a funny place,*
> *A church without a steeple,*
> *Houses made of old ships wrecked,*
> *And most peculiar people."*
>
> Welsh Academy Encyclopaedia of Wales

More information: An informative essay about Mumbles can be found in John Davies, *Wales: 100 Places to See Before You Die* (Y Lolfa, 2010).

Modern moonlight: *Swansea's architecturally striking 'Sail Bridge' (upstream from the main route)*

may attract your attention (besides those in the Mumbles itself): Ripples Café and the West Cross Inn in West Cross, the Woodman in Black Pill, the Pub on the Pond in Singleton, and the Secret Beach Bar and Kitchen at Brynmill. On your way through **Black Pill**, you will also cross the **Clyne River** and pass the entrance to **Clyne Valley Country Park**.

5 After crossing the Clyne, you rejoin **Route 4 of the National Cycle Network**. This will take you to the very end of the section, though the alternative route is recommended.

Alternative route: *A short parallel route along the beach*

If the tide allows, once you've crossed the footbridge over the Clyne river, you can turn right off the cycle route and walk along the beach to the Marina Towers Observatory.

6 Eventually, the **official route** on the cycle path moves away from the main road, bearing right near a children's play area on the beach. The path then continues past **Swansea Civic Centre** to join **Marine Walk**, a pedestrianised road lined with high-rise flats in the city's **Maritime Quarter**. A left turn at the **Marina Towers Observatory** (also known as the Tower Ecliptic) will take you directly to **Swansea Marina** and the 👁 **National Waterfront Museum**.

However, the main route continues ahead. After passing to the right of a parking area, the path reaches the **River Tawe**. Follow the river to the left, where the impressive pedestrian and cyclist **Trafalgar Bridge** crosses the river downsteam from the **Tawe Barrage**. The Coast Path continues on the far side of the river, but this section and guide end here.

Waterfront Museum

Housed in a former dockside warehouse built in 1902, the National Waterfront Museum tells the story of Wales's industrial and maritime heritage. On show are major inventions and devices that transformed transport and industry in Wales and the world. In the Warehouse gallery, a mix of traditional and interactive displays explain the role of industry in shaping the lives of the people of Wales.

Welsh coastal place names

Welsh place names are as much a part of Wales's cultural distinctiveness as its mountains, sheep or rugged coast. To the English visitor, they may appear strangely foreign, confusing or simply unpronounceable. And yet, once carefully unravelled, they can tell us all sorts of fascinating things about a place — its landscape, character and history. Even these few common place name elements should help bring the Wales Coast Path alive.

Aber	river mouth, estuary	*Ab-er*
Afon	river	*Av-on*
Bad	ferry, boat	*Bad*
Bae	bay	*Bai*
Cae	field, enclosure	*Kai*
Carreg	stone, rock	*Kar-reg*
Cawl	sea kale	*Kowl*
Cei	quay	*Kay*
Cilfach	cove, creek	*Kil-vakh*
Clegyr	rock, cliff	*Kleg-ir*
Culfor	strait	*Kil-vor*
Din/dinas	citadel; hillfort; fortified hill	*Deen/Deen-as*
Dŵr/dwfr	water	*Doer/Doo-vr*
Dyffryn	valley; bottom	*Duff-ryn*
Eglwys	church	*Eg-looees*
Ffynnon	well; spring; fountain; source	*Fun-on*
Goleudy	lighthouse	*Gol-ay-dee*
Glan	shore	*Glan*
Gwymon	seaweed	*Gwi-mon*
Harbwr	harbour	*Haboor*
Heli	salt water, brine	*Hel-lee*

Walking towards Worms Head, on the Gower

Llech	flat stone, flagstone, slate	*Th-lekh*
Maen	stone; standing stone	*Mine*
Môr	sea, ocean	*More*
Morfa	sea marsh, salt marsh	*Mor-va*
Moryd	estuary, channel	*Mor-rid*
Ogof	cave	*Og-ov*
Parrog	flat land by the sea	*Par-rog*
Penrhyn	headland	*Pen-rin*
Pigyn	point	*Pig-in*
Pont/bont	bridge, arch	*Pont/Bont*
Porth	harbour	*Porth*
Pwll	pool, pit	*Pooth*
Tafol	dock	*Tav-ol*
Ton/don	wave	*Ton/Don*
Traeth	beach	*Treye-th*
Trwyn	nose; point, cape	*Troo-een*
Tywyn	sandy shore sand dunes	*Tow-in*
Ynys	island	*Un-iss*

"Wales, where the past still lives. Where every place has its tradition, every name its poetry ..."

Matthew Arnold, *On the Study of Celtic Literature*, 1866

Useful Information

Wales Coast Path

Comprehensive information about all sections of the Wales Coast Path can be found on the official website at: **www.walescoastpath.gov.uk** and **www.walescoastpath.co.uk**.

'Visit Wales'

The Visit Wales website covers everything from accommodation to attractions. For information on the area covered by this book, read the relevant sections on **www.visitwales.com**

Carmarthen Bay and the Gower Peninsula

For local information about Carmarthenshire, from what to do to eating out, see **www.discovercarmarthenshire.com**. To learn more about Swansea and the Gower Peninsula, visit **www.visitswanseabay.com** or **www.gowerholidays.com**

Tourist Information Centres

The main TICs around Carmarthen Bay and the Gower Peninsula provide free information on everything from accommodation and travel to what's on and walking advice.

Saundersfoot   01437 776050   saundersfootlibrary@pembrokeshire.gov.uk
Carmarthen   01267 231557   carmarthentic@carmarthenshire.gov.uk
Llanelli   01554 777744   discoverycentre@carmarthenshire.gov.uk

Where to stay

There's lots of accommodation close to the Wales Coast Path around Carmarthen Bay and the Gower Peninsula, from campsites and B&Bs to holiday cottages and hotels. Tourist Information Centre staff will know what's available locally and can even book for you. **www.visitpembrokeshire.com** and **www.visitswanseabay.com** are good for accommodation listings. Alternatively, book online. Find campsites at **www.campsites.co.uk**

Walking holidays

The following company offers complete walking packages for the Wales Coast Path in Gower, including accommodation, local information, maps, baggage transfer and transport.

Celtic Trails 01291 689774 | **www.celtictrailswalkingholidays.co.uk**

Train and buses

For public transport information across Wales, see **Traveline Cymru** | 0800 464 00 00 | www.traveline.cymru

West Wales Lines trains run from Swansea to Tenby, stopping en-route at Gowerton, Llanelli, Burry Port, Kidwelly, Ferryside, Carmarthen and Saundersfoot. For train times and tickets, see Arriva Trains Wales **www.arrivatrainswales.co.uk** or National Rail Enquiries **www.nationalrail.co.uk**. There is a regular bus service connecting Pendine with Tenby and a number of other bus services radiating from Carmarthen. The Gower Peninsula is served by a variety of bus services radiating from Swansea. For downloadable timetables, use the journey planner on **www.traveline.cymru**

Taxis

Tenby Tenby Taxis 01834 843678 **Carmarthen** Guv's Taxis 07811 111679 **Kidwelly** Kidwelly Cabs 07766 836761 **Llanelli** Andy's Taxis 01554 741373 **Swansea** Data Cabs 01792 474747 | **www.datacabs.com** | contact@datacabs.com

Cycle hire

Burry Port Llanelli & Burry Port Cycles, 47 Station Road | 01269 845656 **Llanelli** Merlin Cycle Tours, North Dock | 01554 756603 | 07875 060815 **Swansea** Action Bikes, 5 St David's Place | 01792 464640 | **www.actionsbikesswansea.co.uk**; The Bike Hub, St Helen's Road | 01792 466944 | **www.swanseabikeshop.blogspot.com**

Cycle repairs

Tenby Cycle Repairs (Cycle Fit), The Old Dairy, Lower Park Road, Tenby. 07817 029997 | tenbycycles@gmail.com

Boat Trips

Tenby Daily trips to Caldey Island (except Sundays) throughout the summer. **www.caldeyislandwales.com**

Saundersfoot A range of pleasure-boat trips, from sport and mackerel fishing to seal watching and coastal cruises. 01834 811027 Saundersfoot Sealife Adventures | 07494 29 39 83 | **www.saundersfootseasafari.co.uk**

Port-Eynon and Mumbles Exhilarating trips along the scenic south Gower coast in a rigid-hulled inflatable boat. 01792 348229 **www.gowercoastadventures.co.uk** info@gowercoastadventures.co.uk

Emergencies

In an emergency, call 999 or 112 and ask for the service you require: Ambulance, Police, Fire or Coastguard. Dyfed Powys Police: 01267 222020; South Wales Police 01656 655555

Tides

Short stretches of the Wales Coast Path and some alternative routes are only accessible on a low or outgoing tide. Check tide times before you go. Tide table booklets are widely available from TICs and local shops for around £1. For today's local tide information for places around Carmarthen Bay and the Gower Peninsula, visit **www.bbc.com/weather/coast-and-sea/tide-tables** and choose your nearest location.

Weather forecasts

For reliable, up-to-date weather forecasts, see **www.bbc.com/weather** or **www.metoffice.gov.uk/weather/forecast/uk**

Annual events

The Laugharne Weekend: April

Gower Walking Festival: June

Carmarthen River Festival: July

Gower Show, Reynoldston: first Sunday in August

The Dylan Thomas Festival, Swansea: 27 October to 9 November

Tenby's Annual Boxing Day Swim & Raft Race

Further reading

Top 10 Walks: Wales Coast Path: Carmarthen Bay & Gower, by Harri Roberts. Northern Eye Books ISBN 978-1-908632-16-6

Gower, by Nigel Jenkins and David Pearl. Gomer Press ISBN 978-1-848510-52-4

Wales Coast Path: Official Guides

The **Official Guides** to the **Wales Coast Path** are endorsed by Natural Resources Wales, the Welsh government body which developed and manage the path. The guides break the Wales Coast Path into seven main sections, giving long-distance and local walkers everything they need to enjoy all 870 miles of this world-class route.

North Wales Coast
Chester to Bangor
ISBN: 978-0-9559625-1-6

Isle of Anglesey
Circuit from Menai Bridge
ISBN: 978-1-902512-15-0

Llŷn Peninsula
Bangor to Porthmadog
ISBN: 978-1-908632-24-1

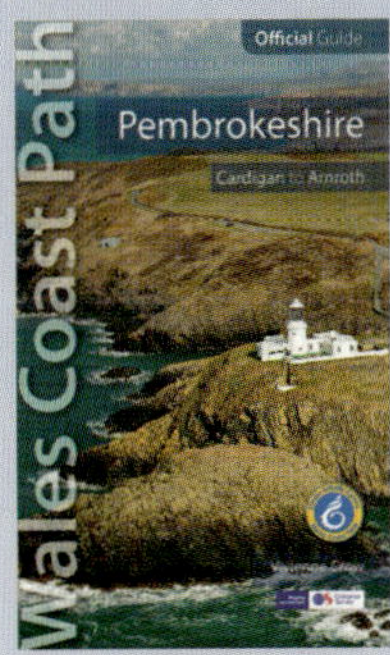

Pembrokeshire
Cardigan to Amroth
ISBN: 978-1-908632-23-4

Carmarthen Bay &
Gower *Tenby to Swansea*
ISBN: 978-1-908632-26-5

South Wales Coast
Swansea to Chepstow
ISBN: 978-1-908632-27-2

Wales Coast Path: Top 10 Walks

Award-winning pocket-size walking guides to the most popular, easy circular walks along key sections of the Wales Coast Path. The full series will cover the whole path in ten attractive guides.

Currently available

Top 10 Walks:
Llyn Peninsula
ISBN: 978-1-908632-12-8

Top 10 Walks:
Cardigan Bay North
ISBN: 978-1 908632-13-5

Top 10 Walks:
The Ceredigion Coast
ISBN: 978-1-908632-28-9

Top 10 Walks:
Pembrokeshire North
ISBN: 978-1-908632-29-6

Top 10 Walks:
Pembrokeshire South
ISBN: 978-1 908632-30-2

Top 10 Walks:
Carmarthenshire & Gower
ISBN: 978-1-908632-16-6